Email us at
schoolhome.kids@gmail.com

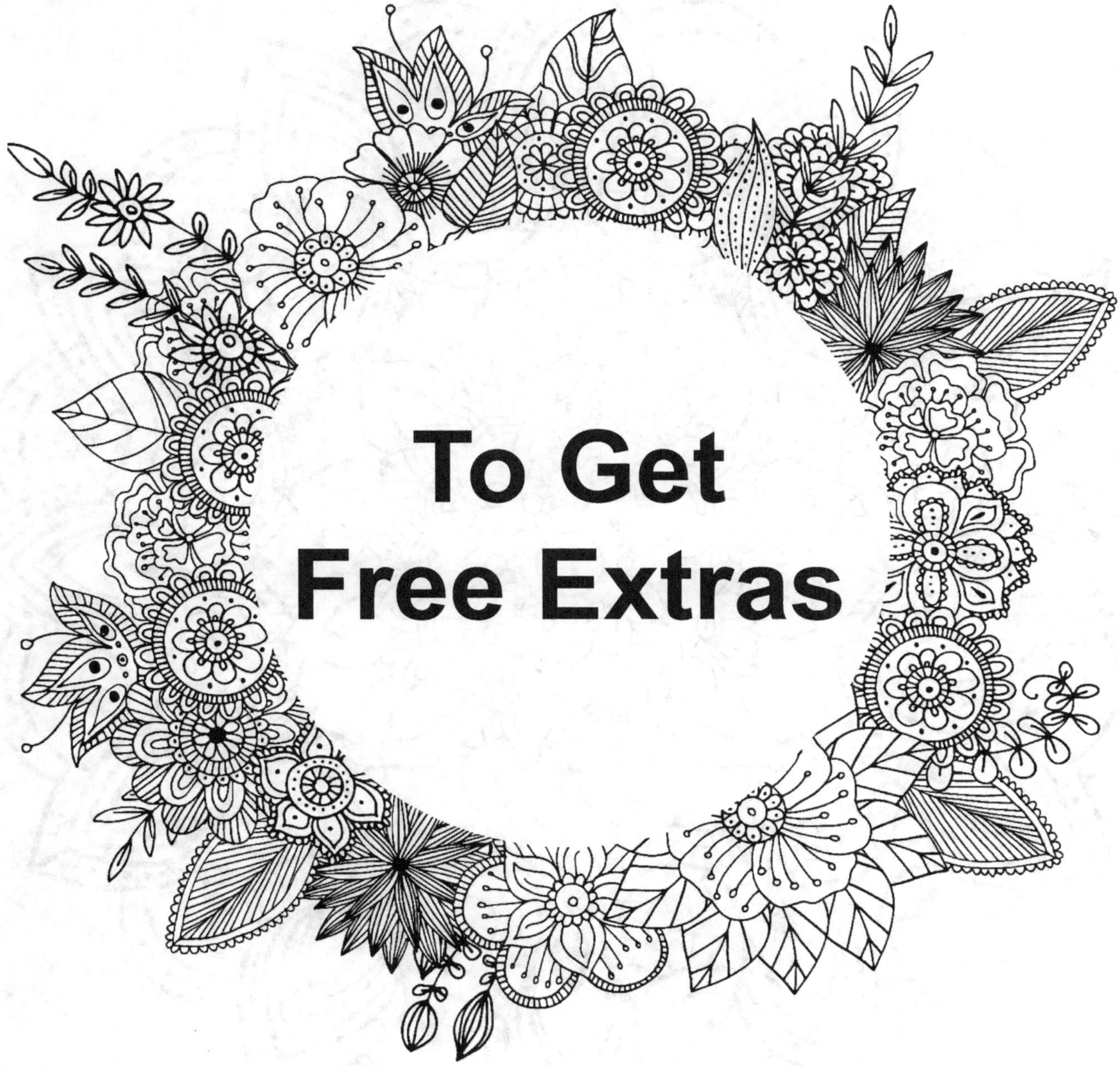

To Get Free Extras

just titre the email
- Adult Coloring Book -
And we will send some extra surprises your way !.

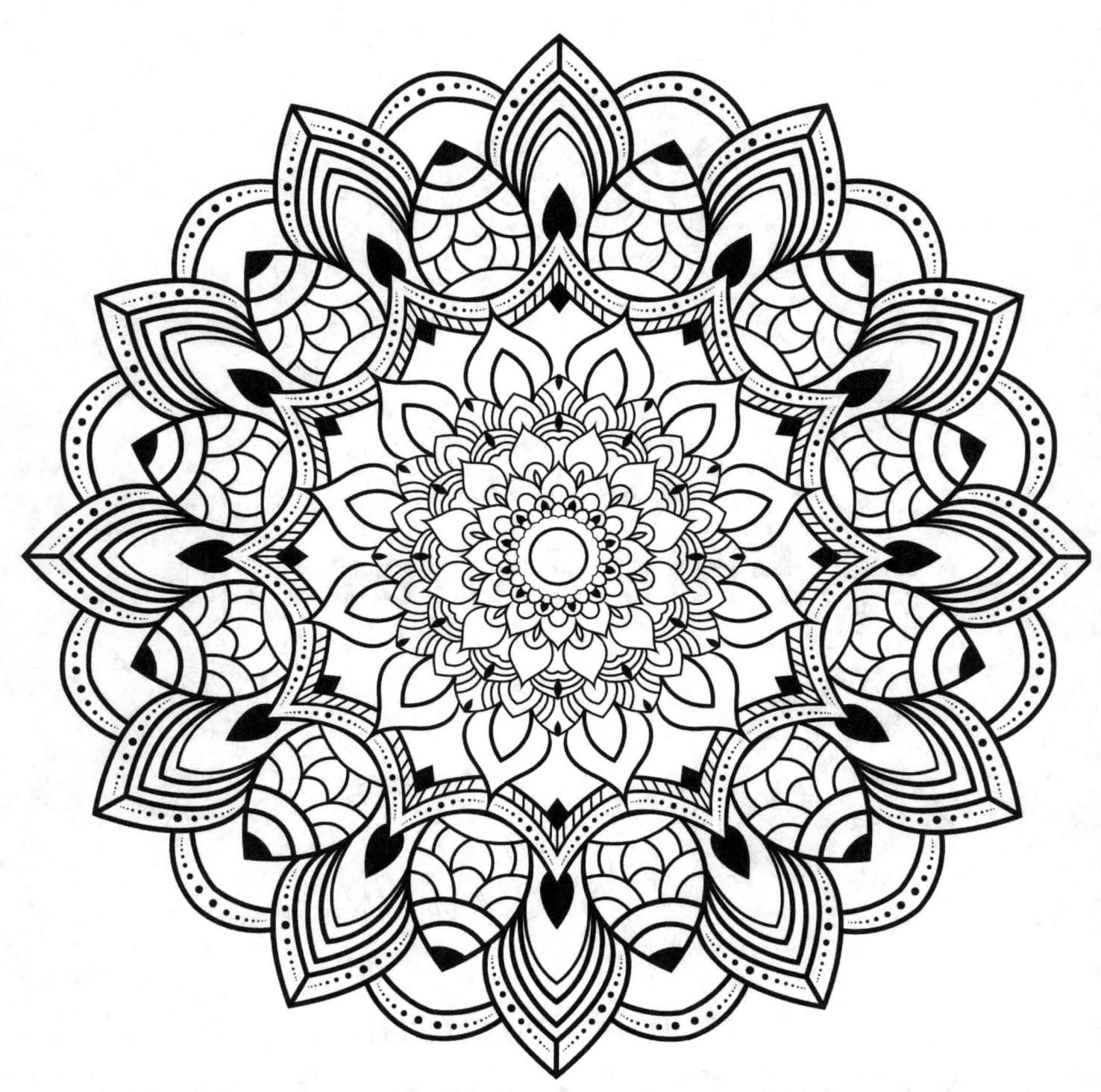

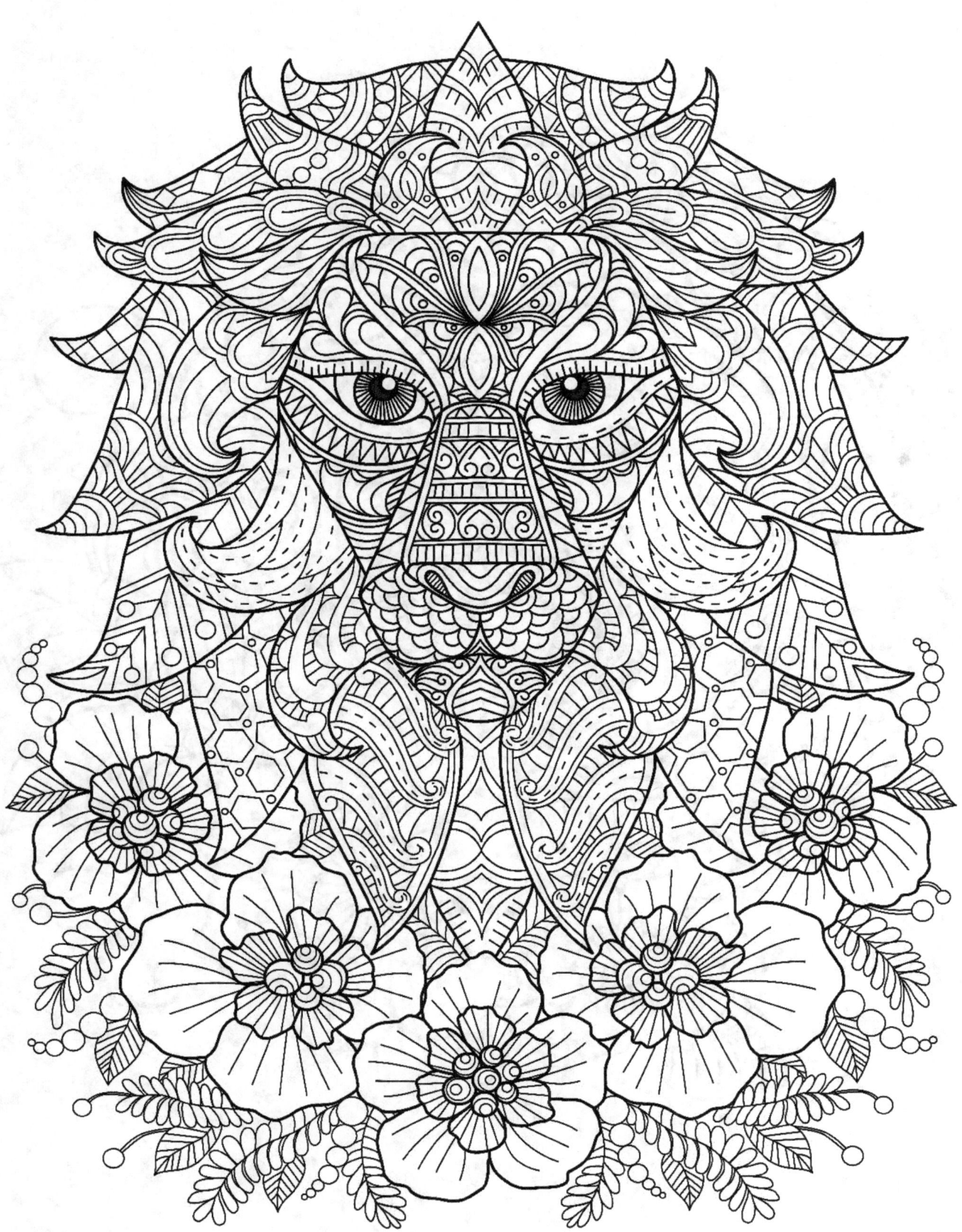

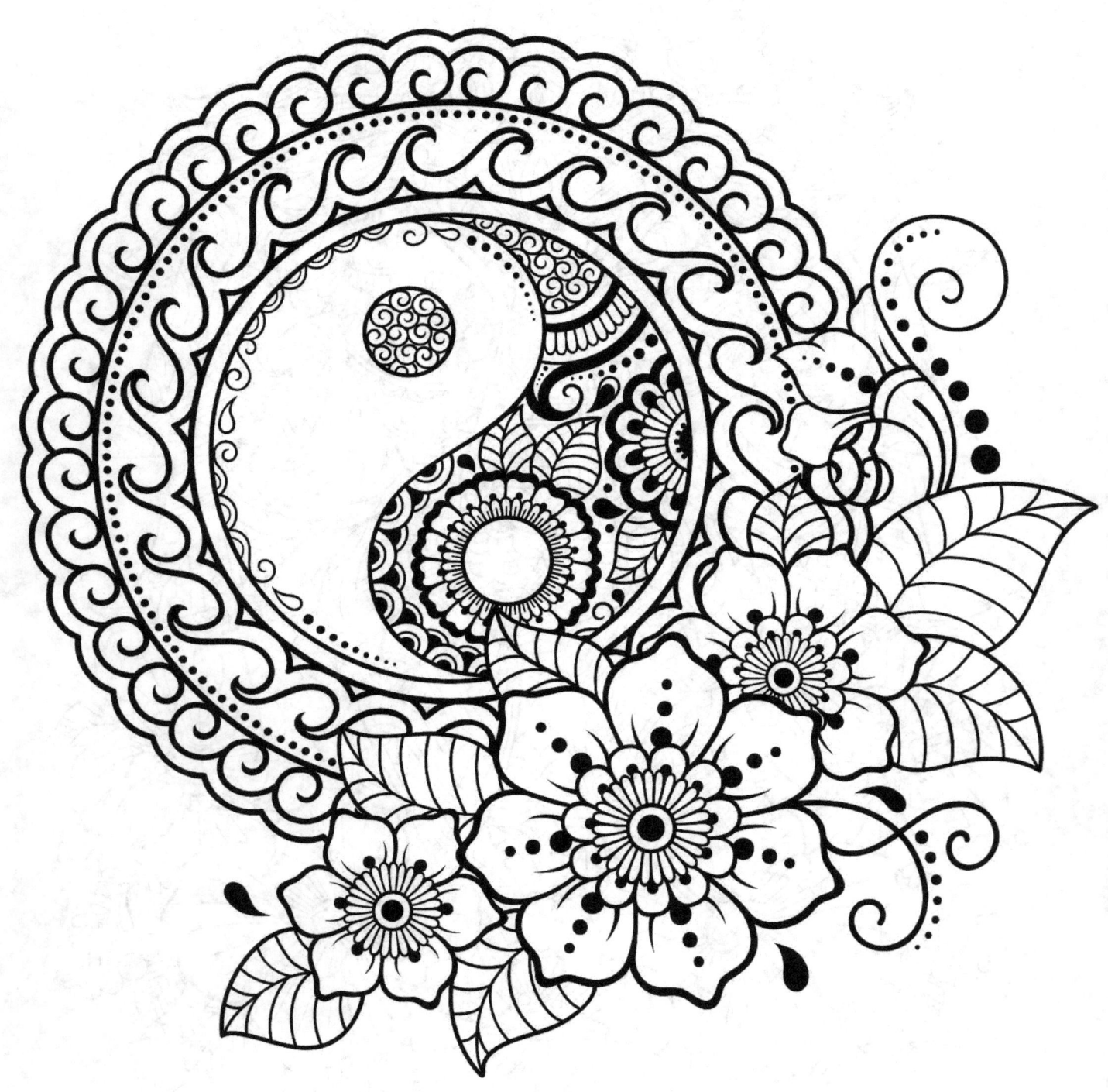

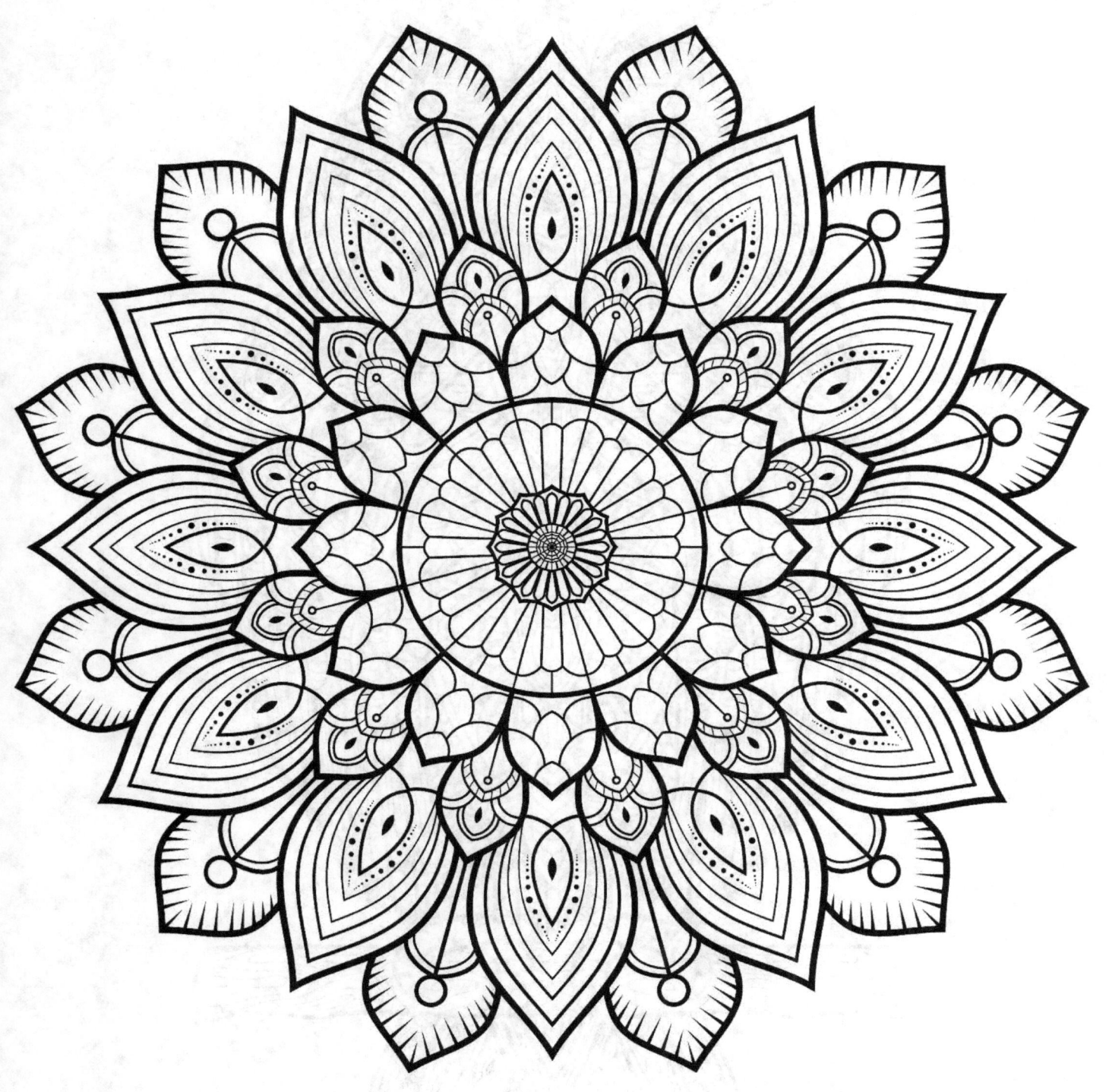

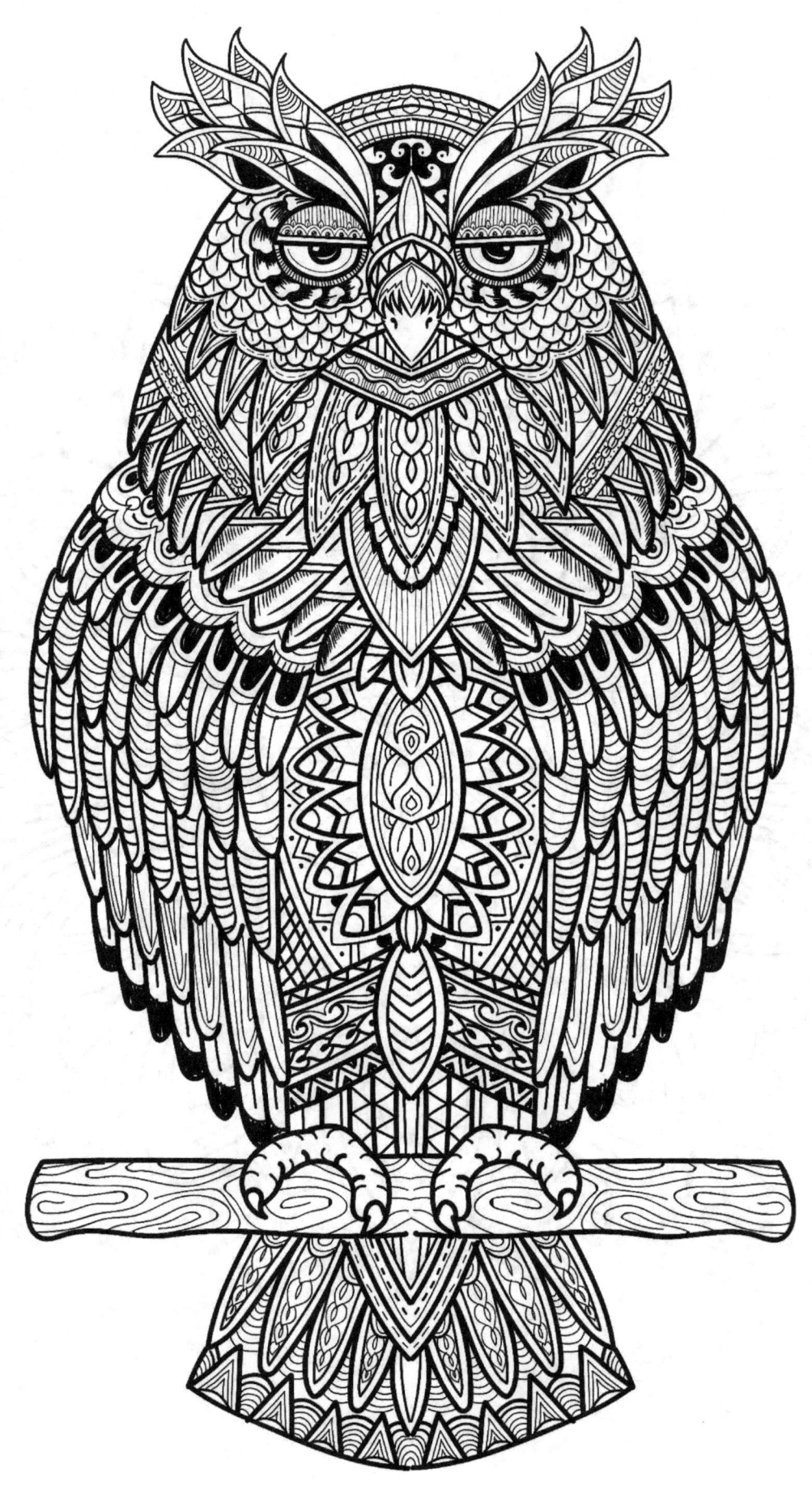

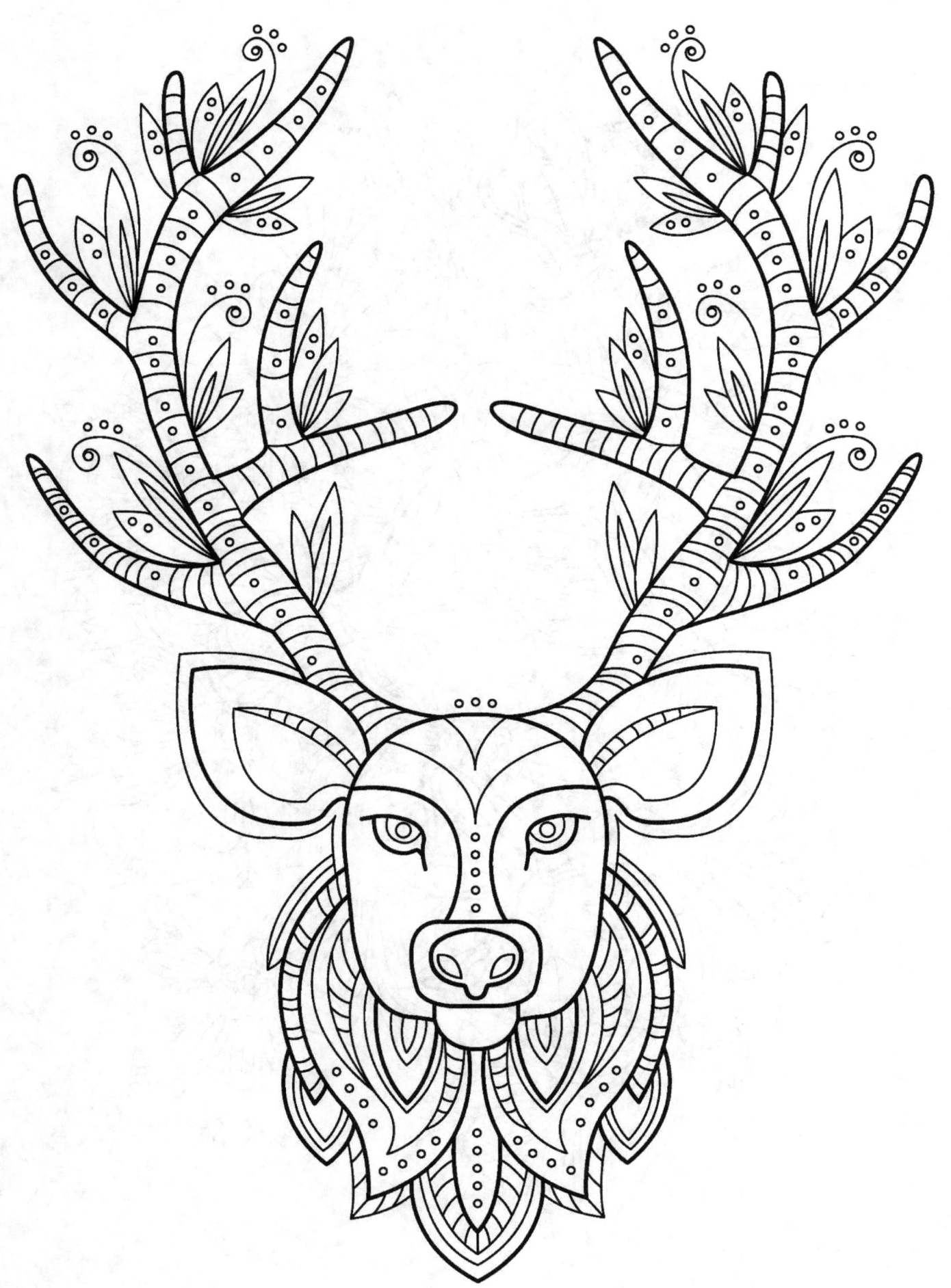

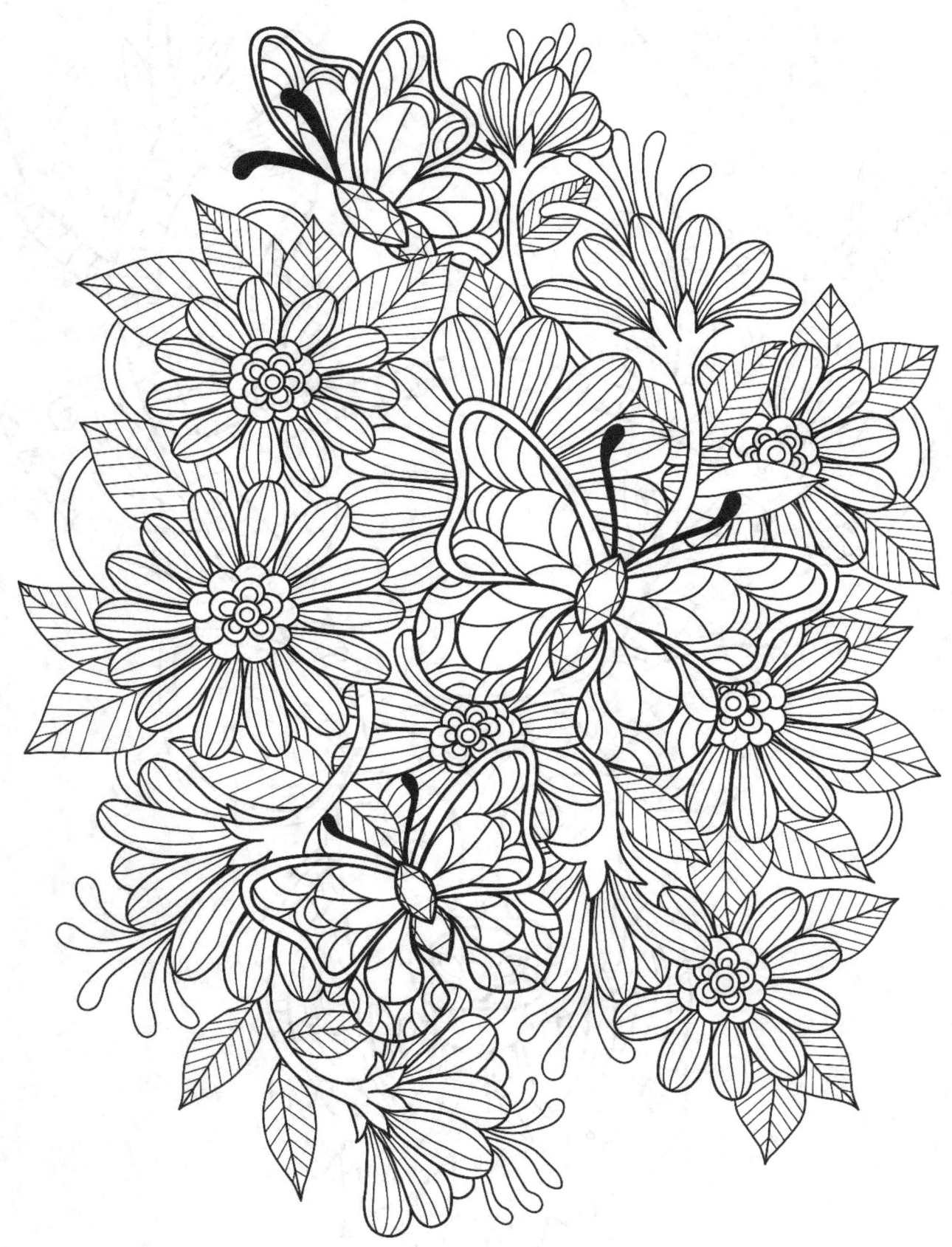

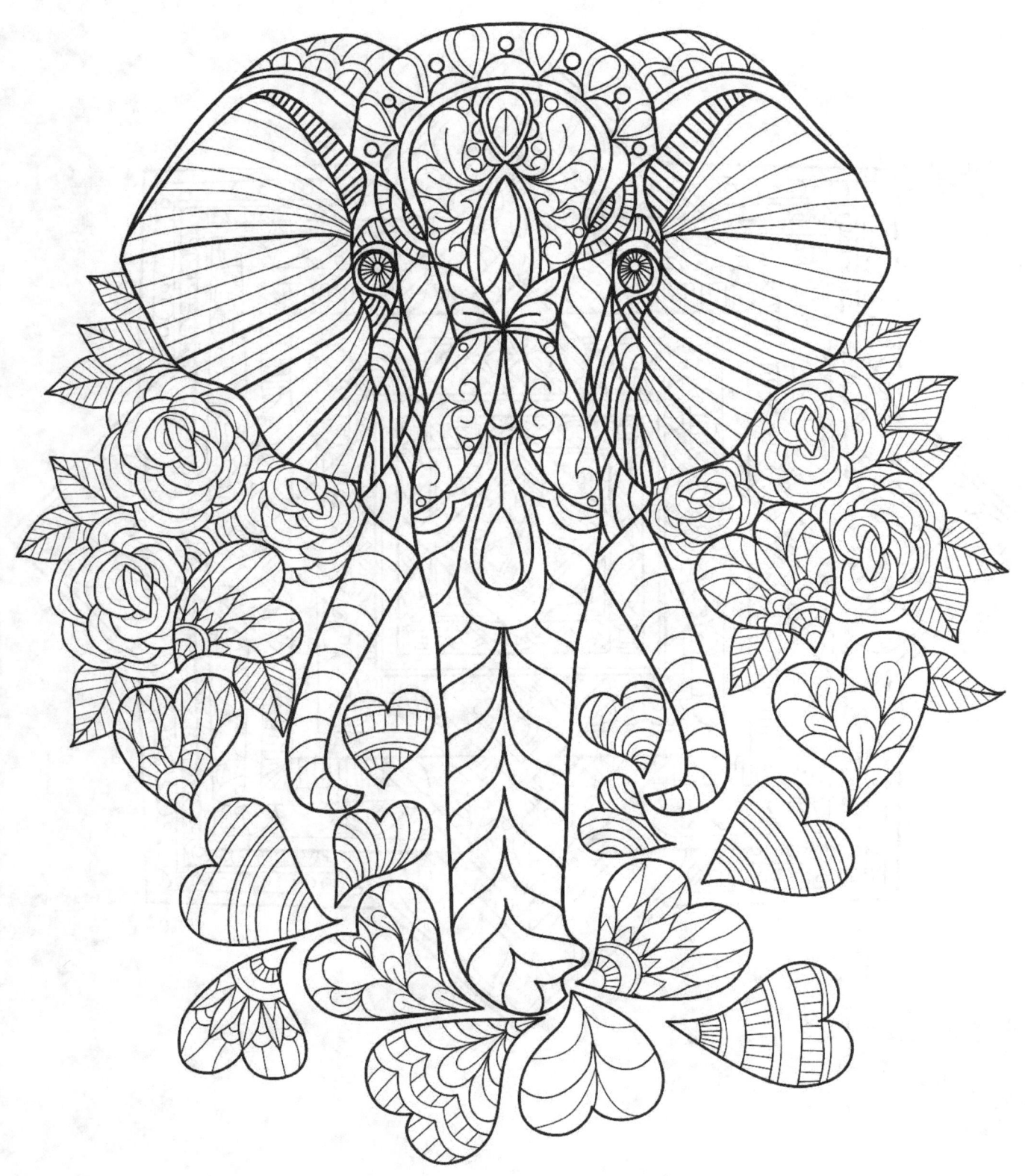

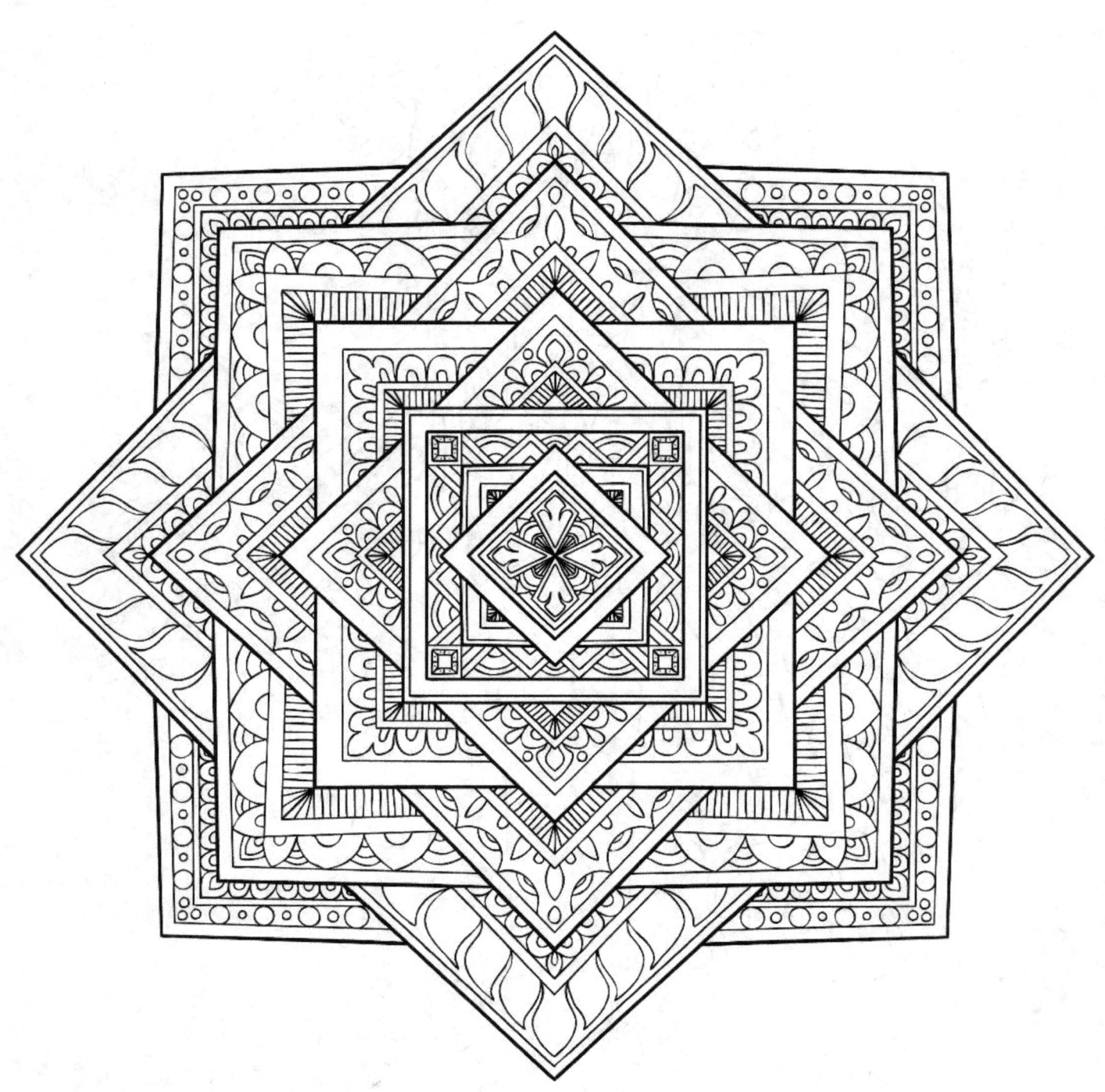

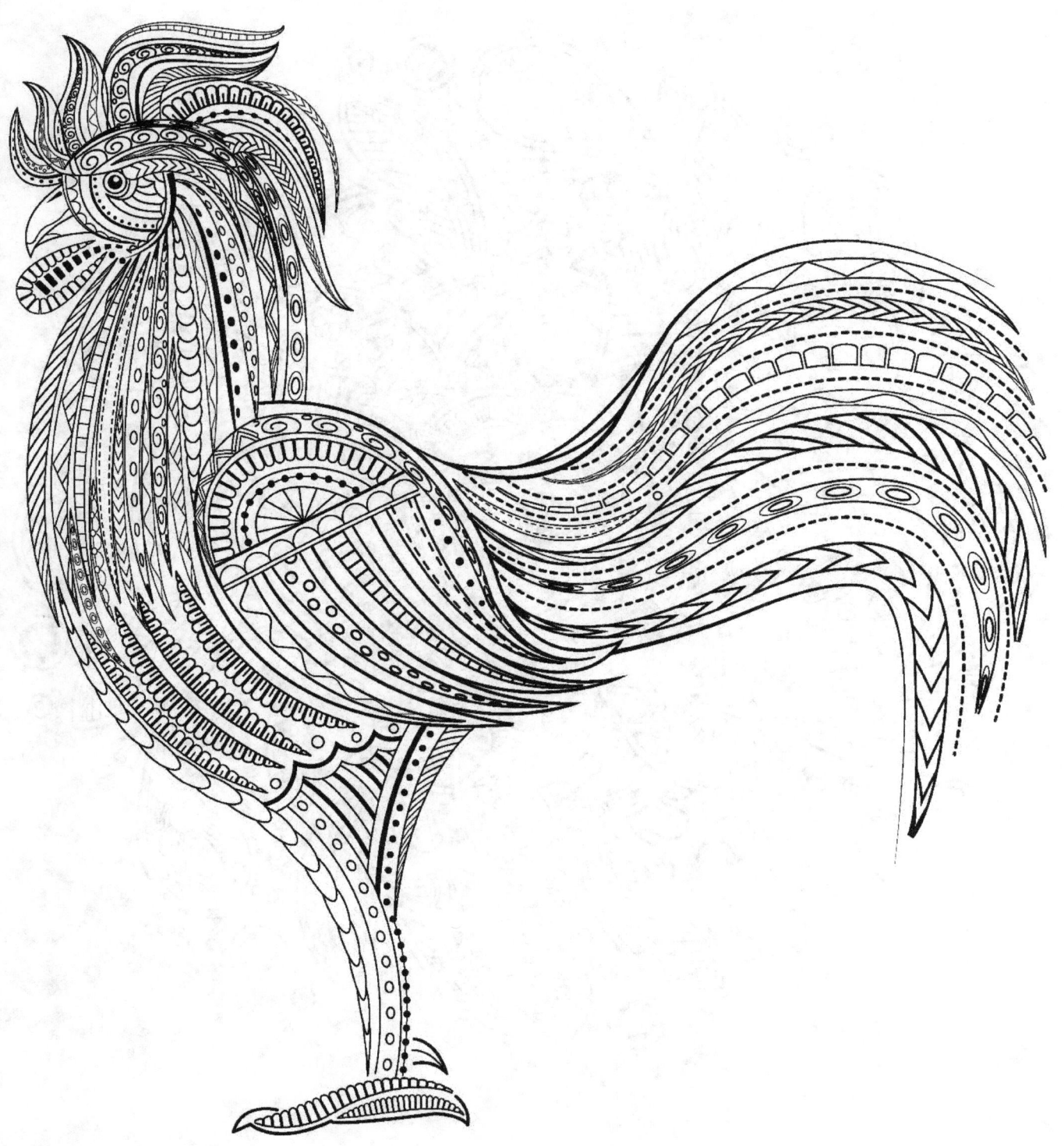

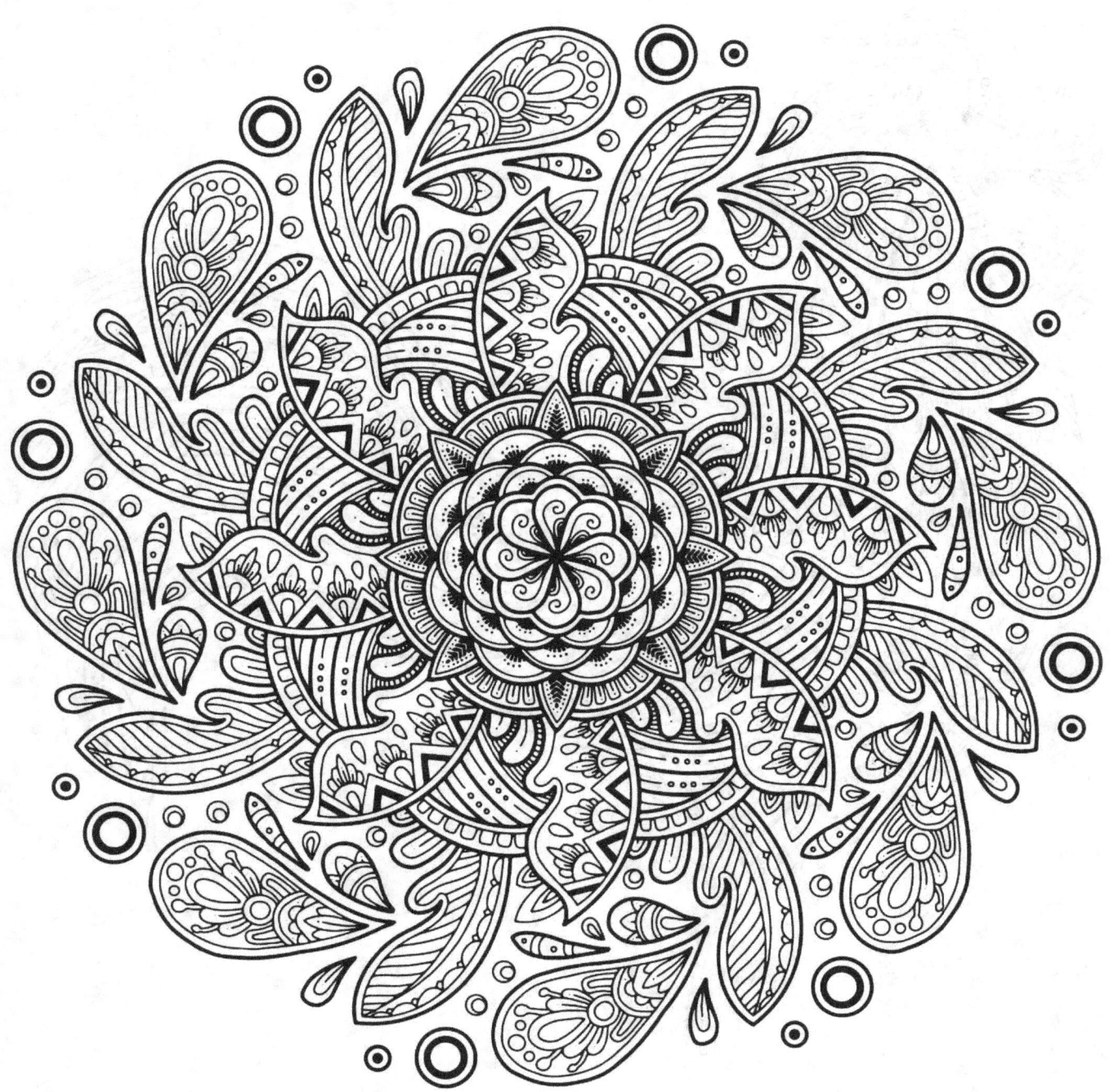

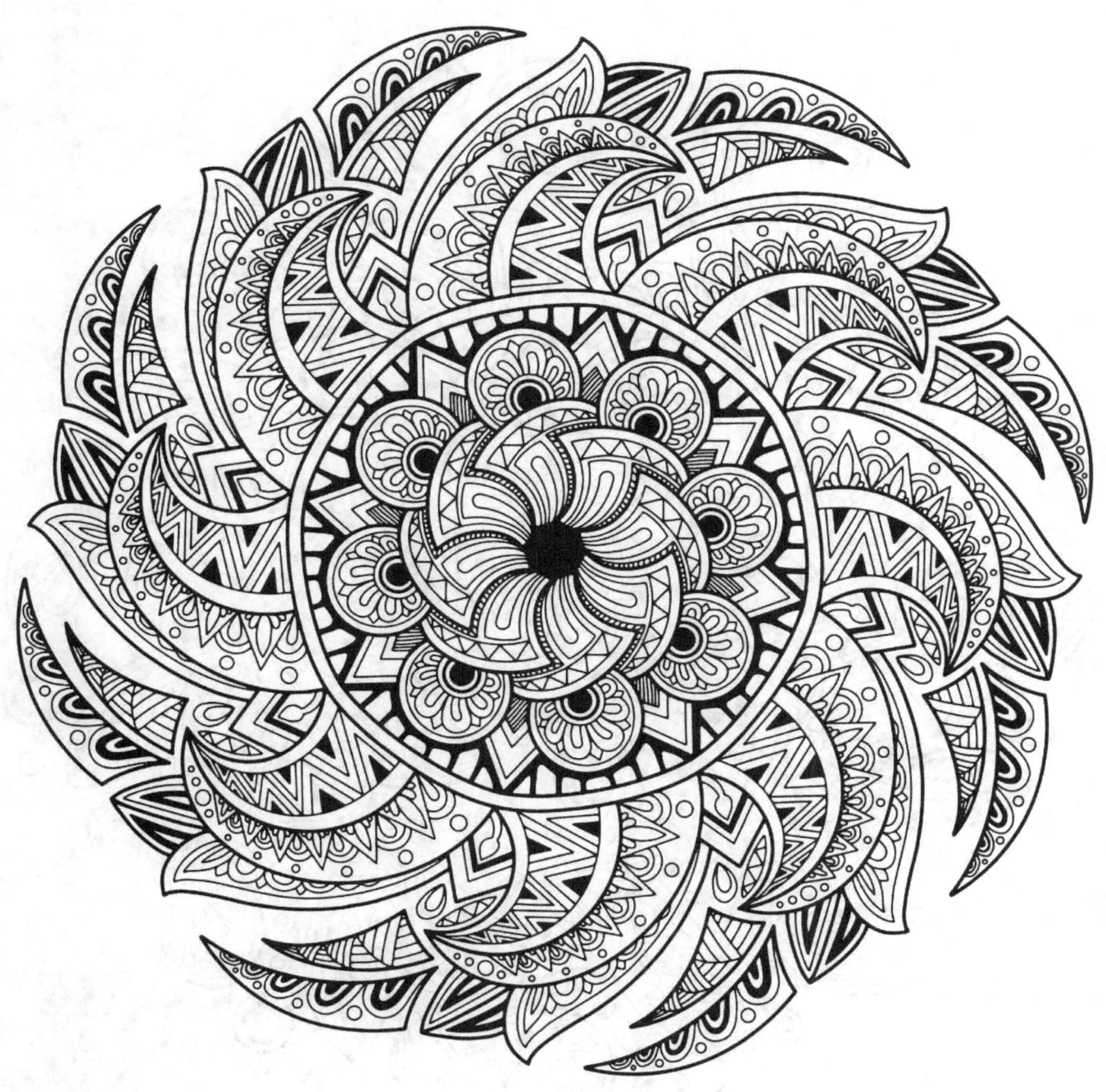

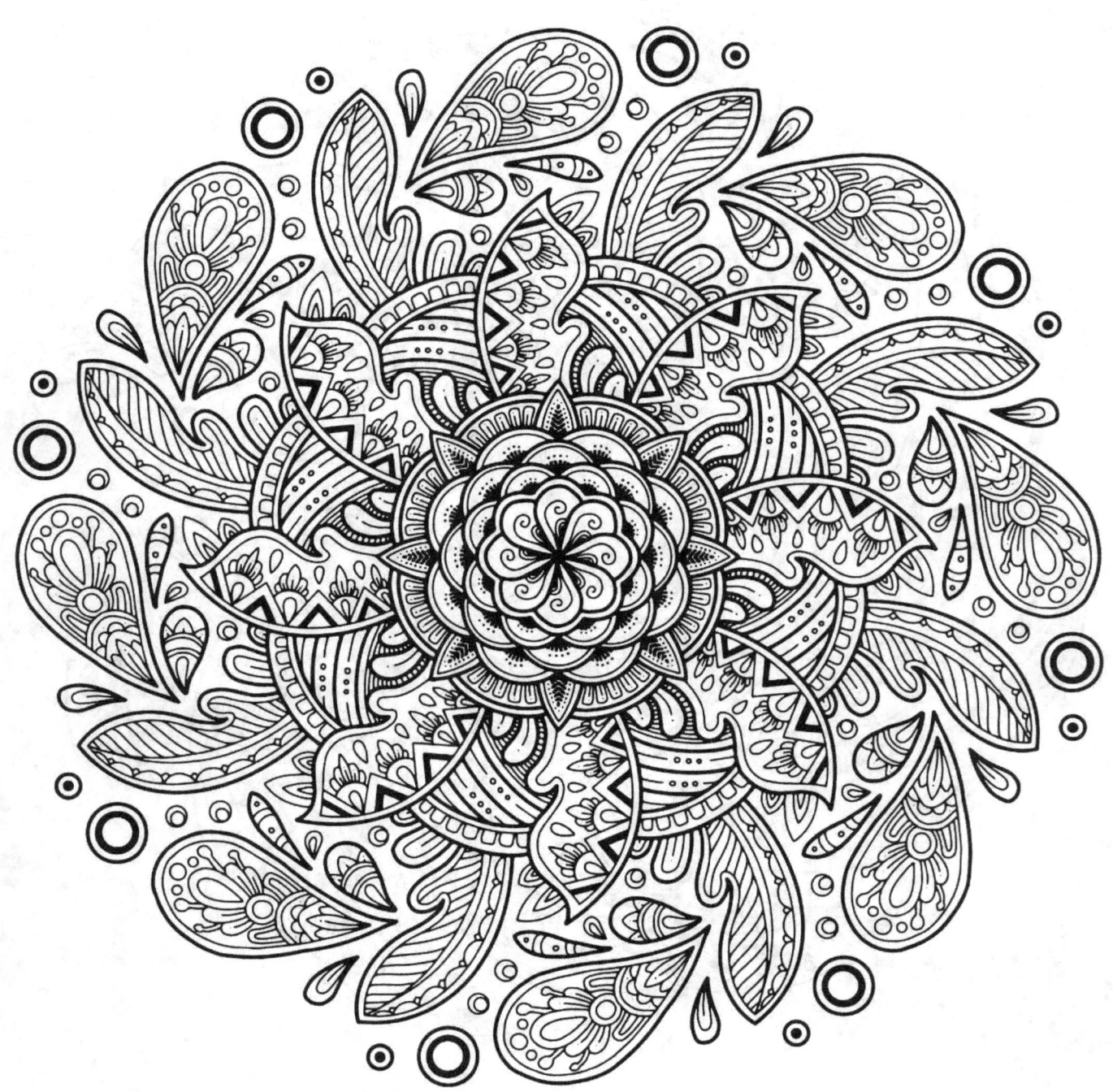

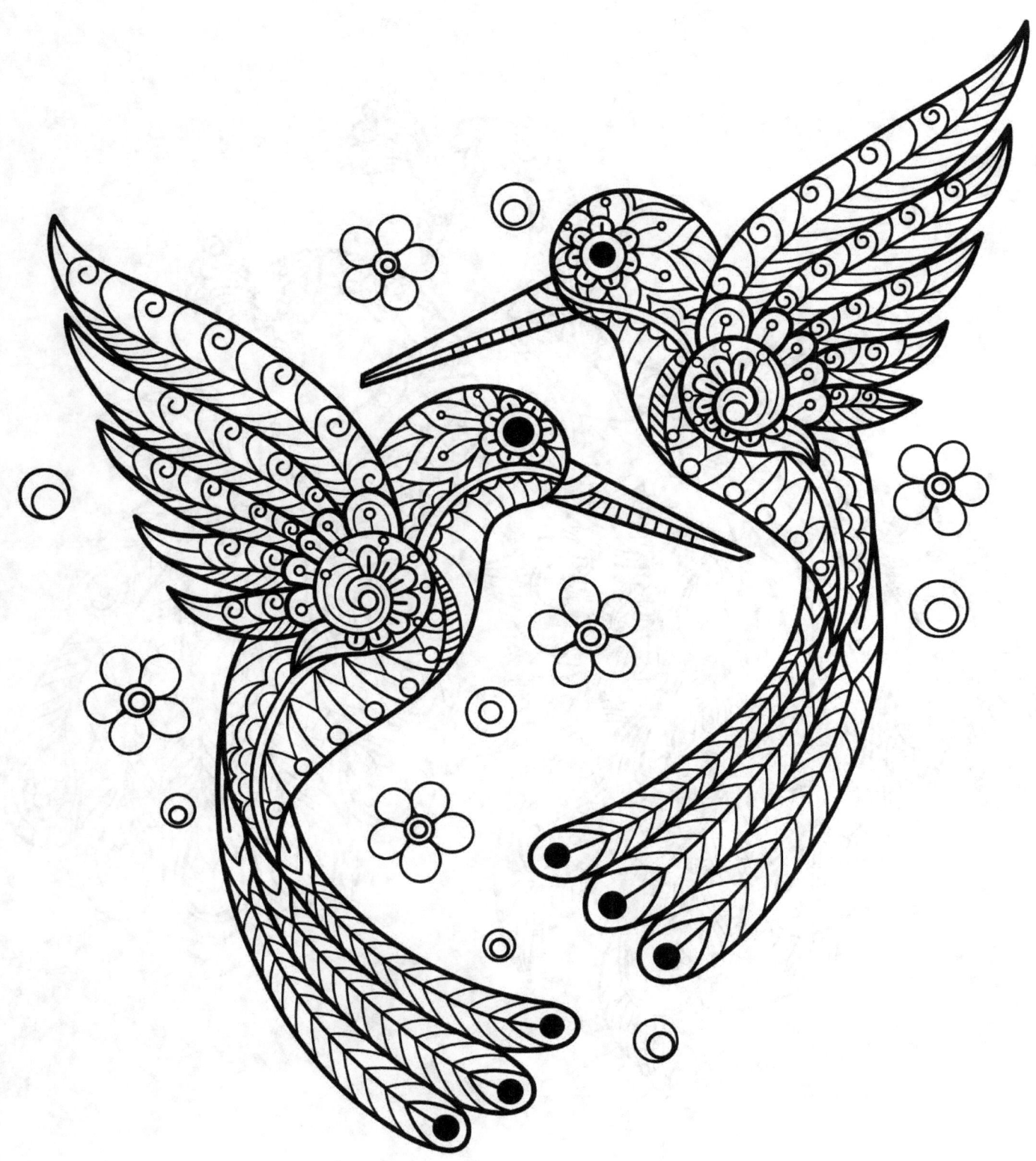

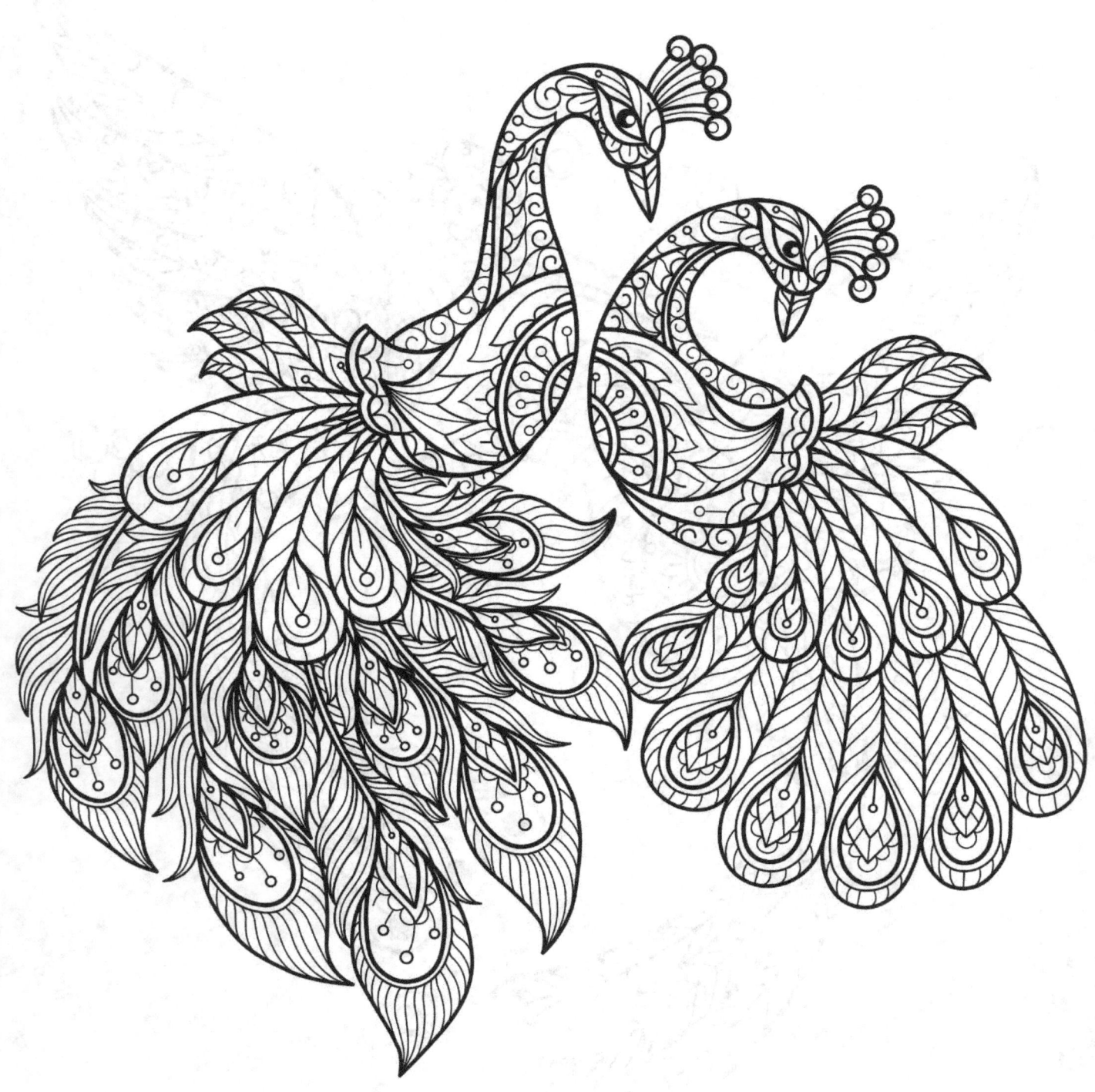

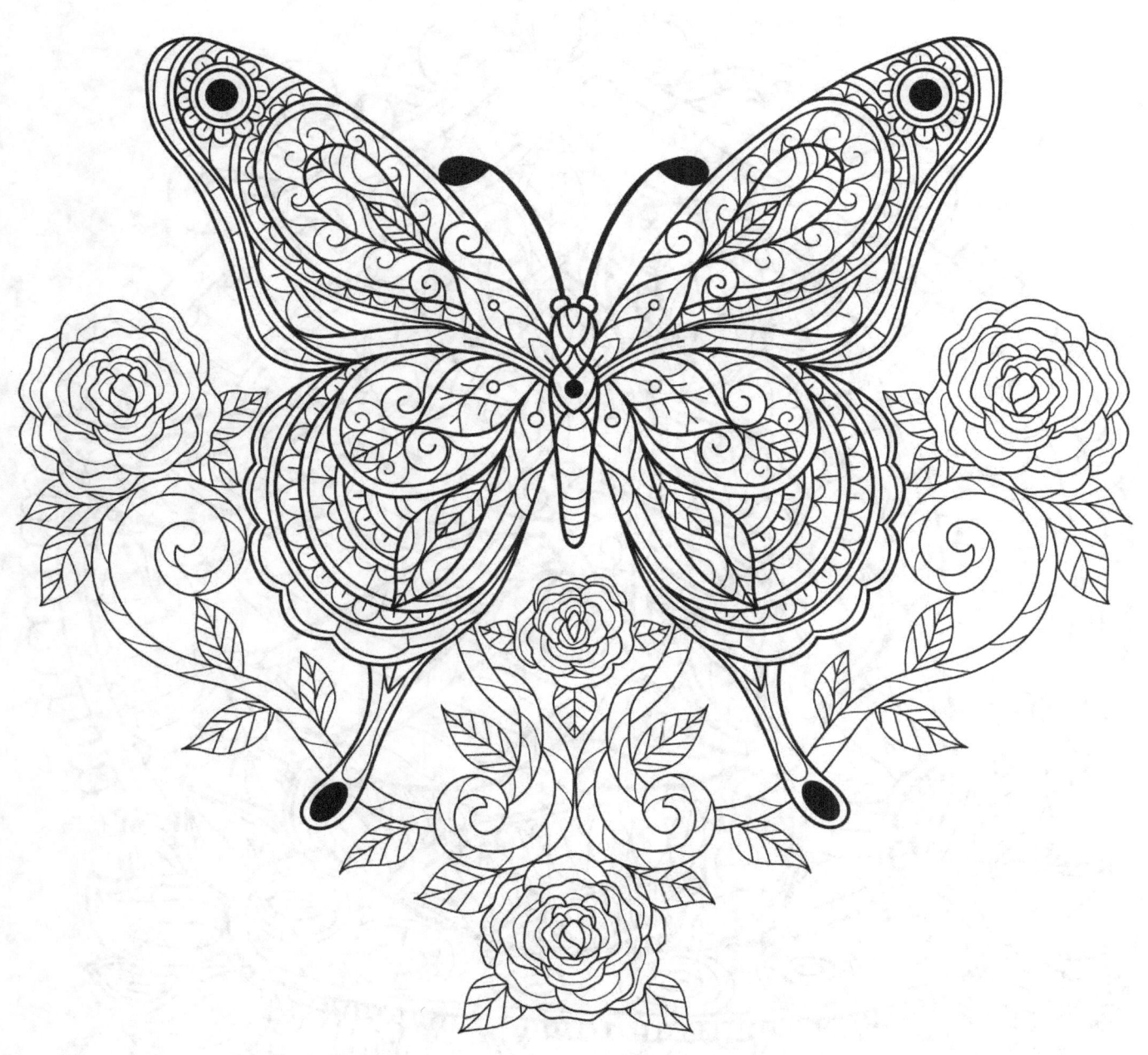

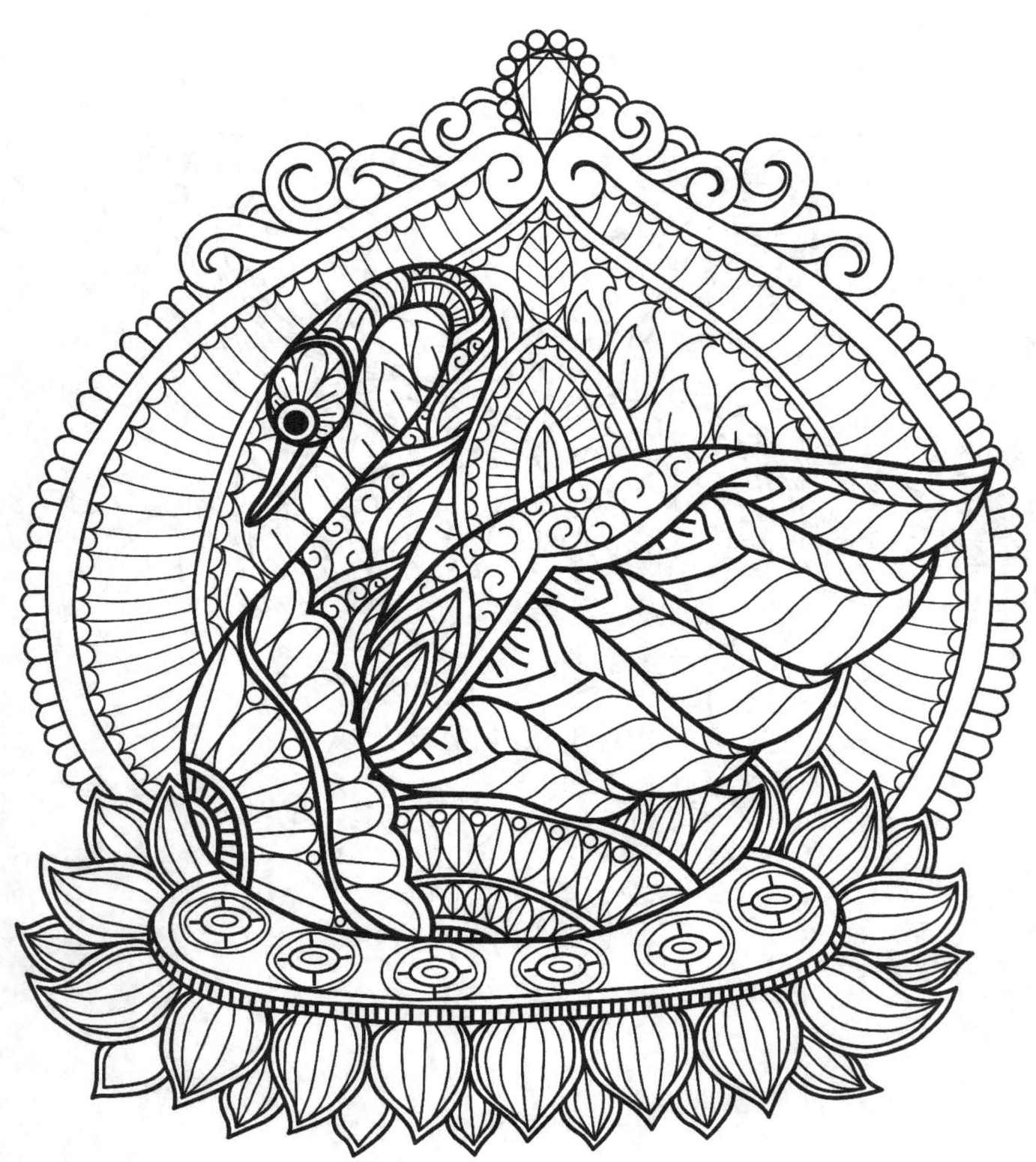

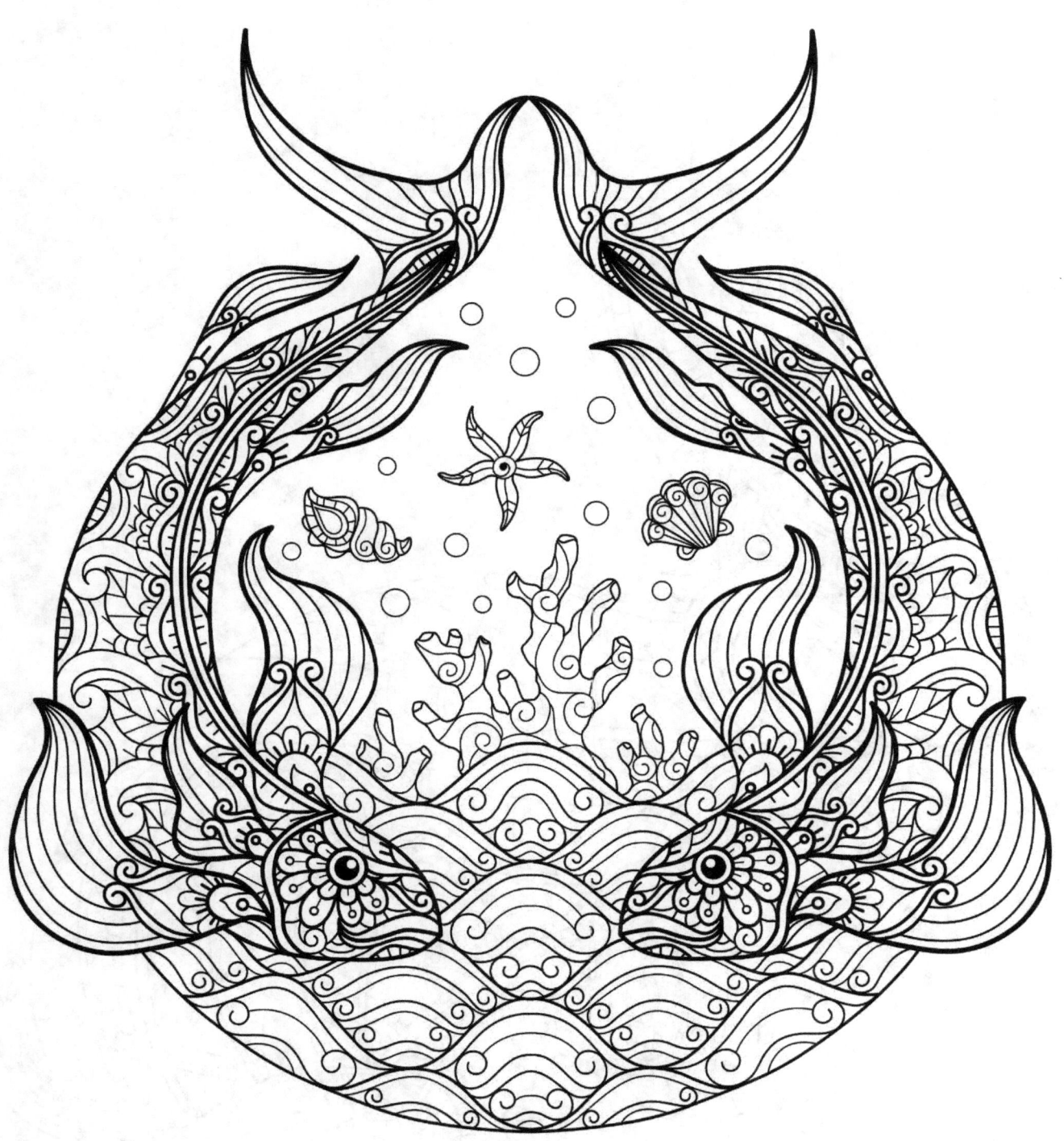

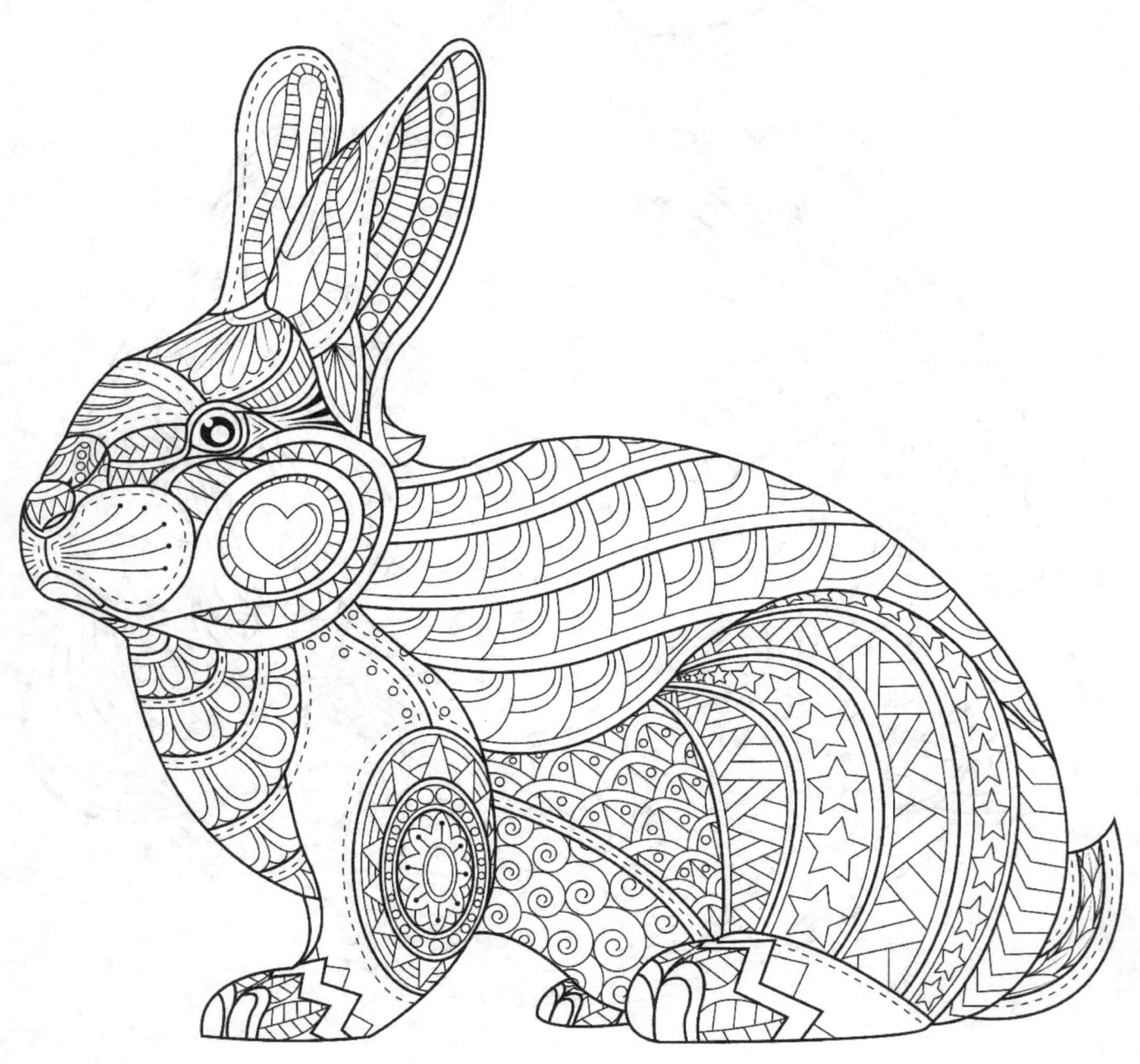

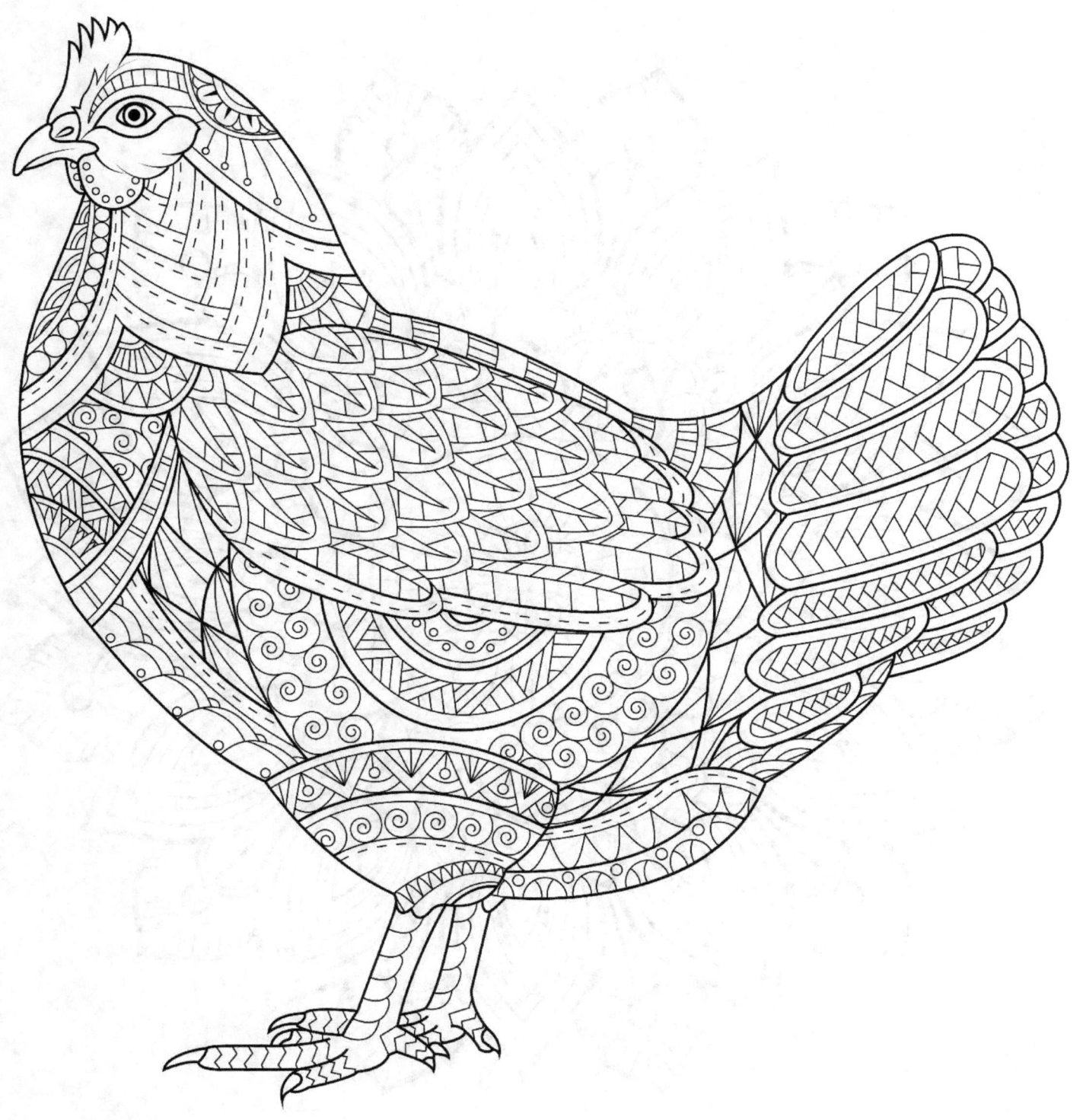

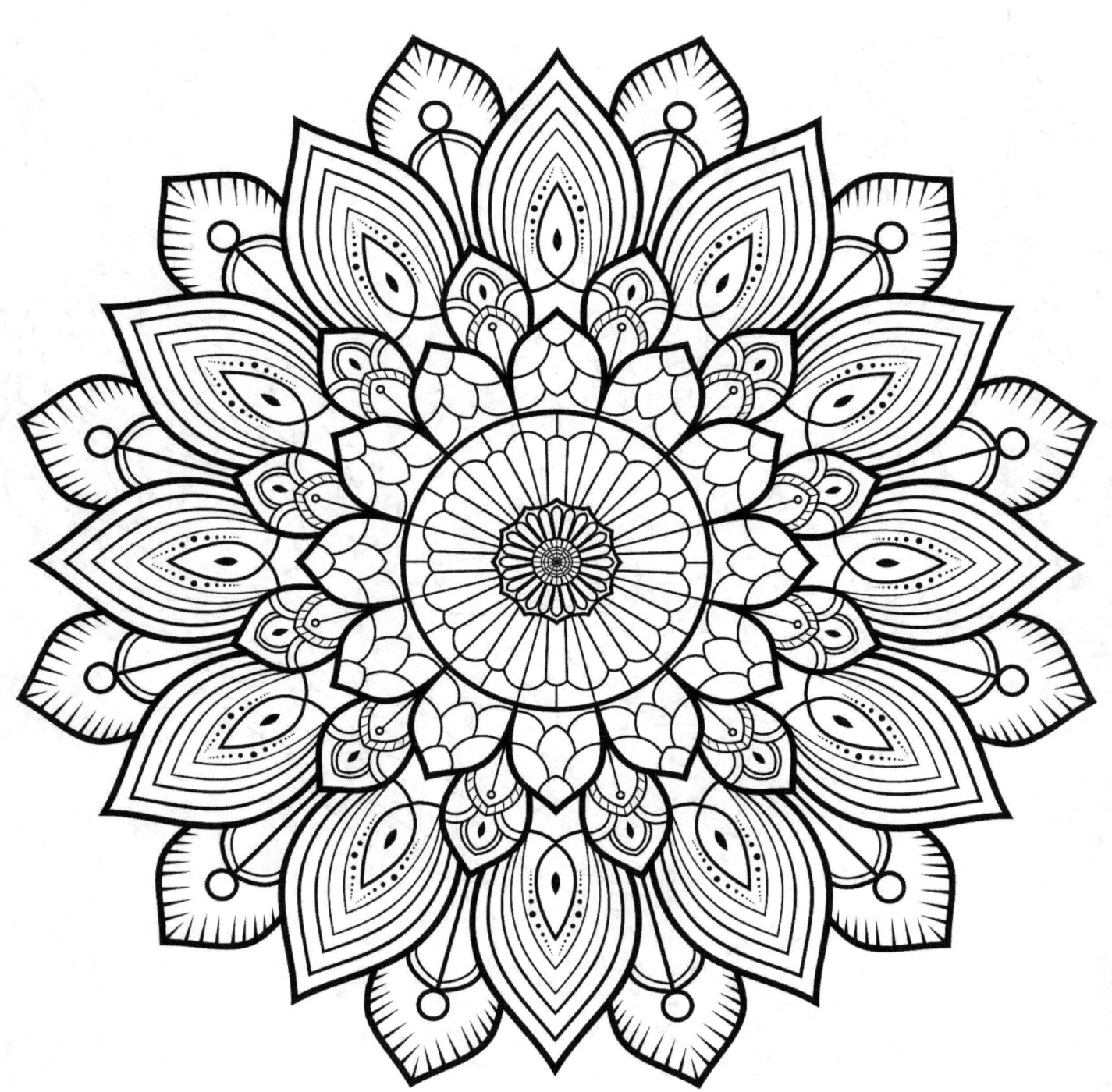

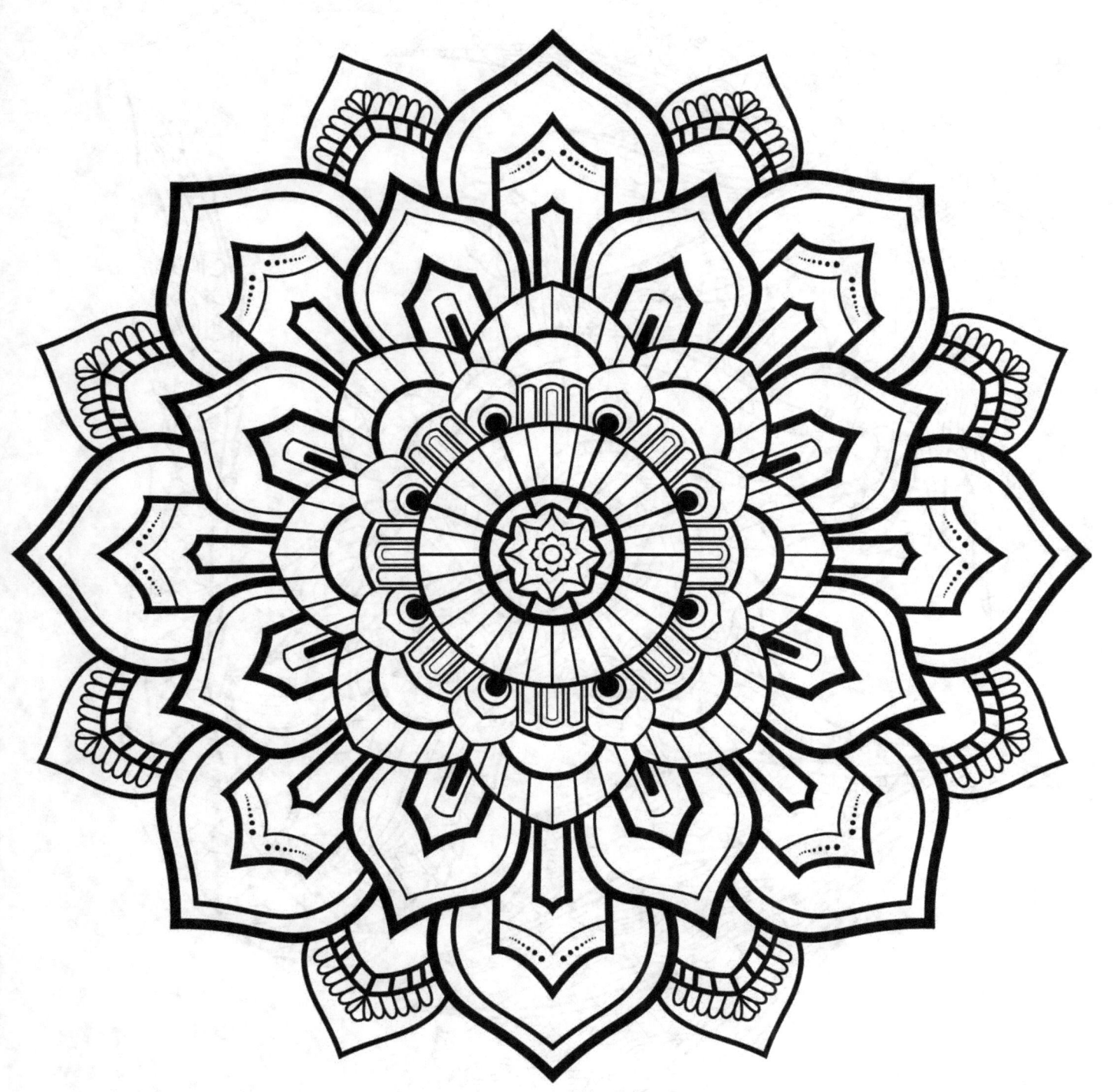

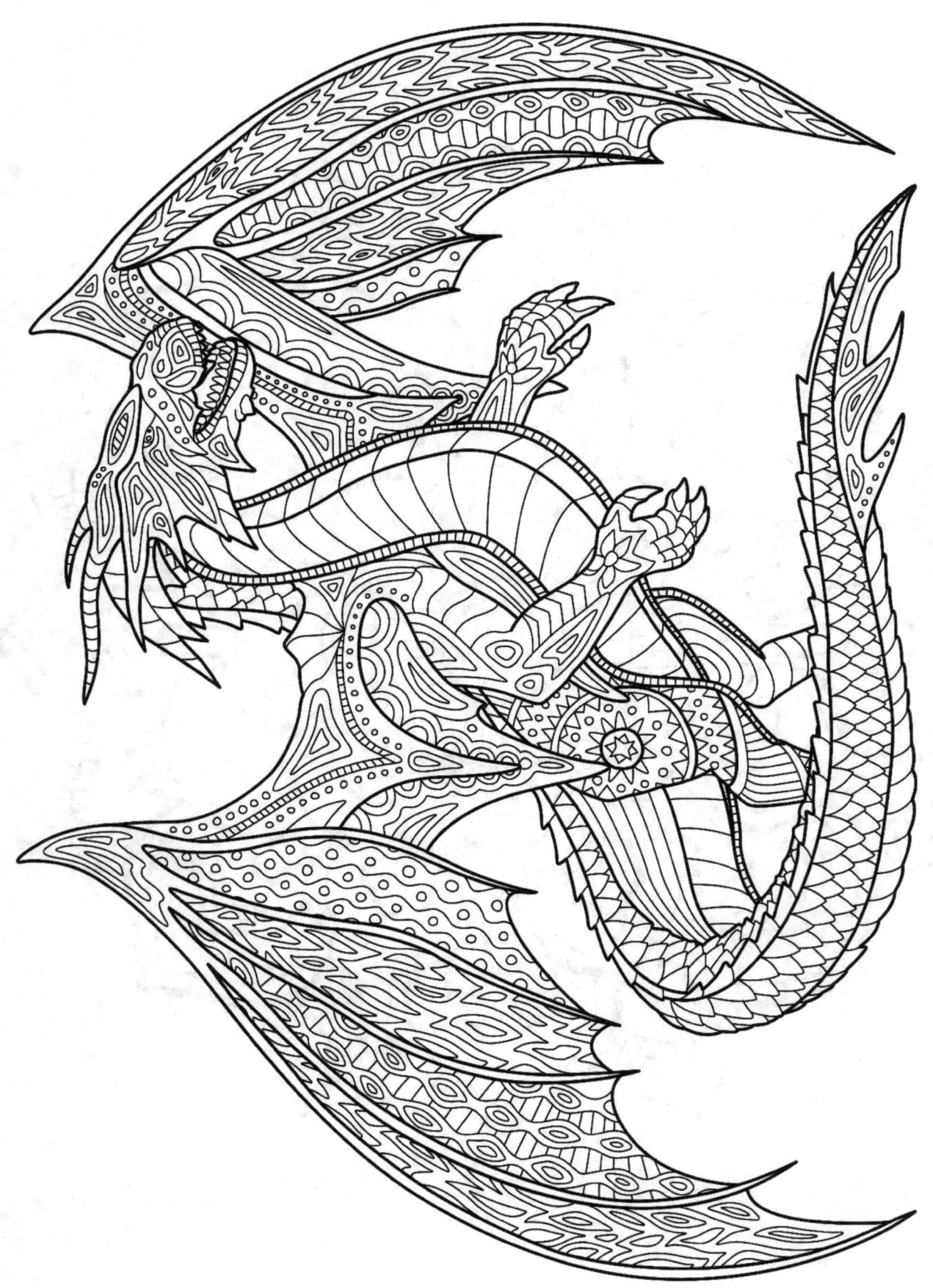

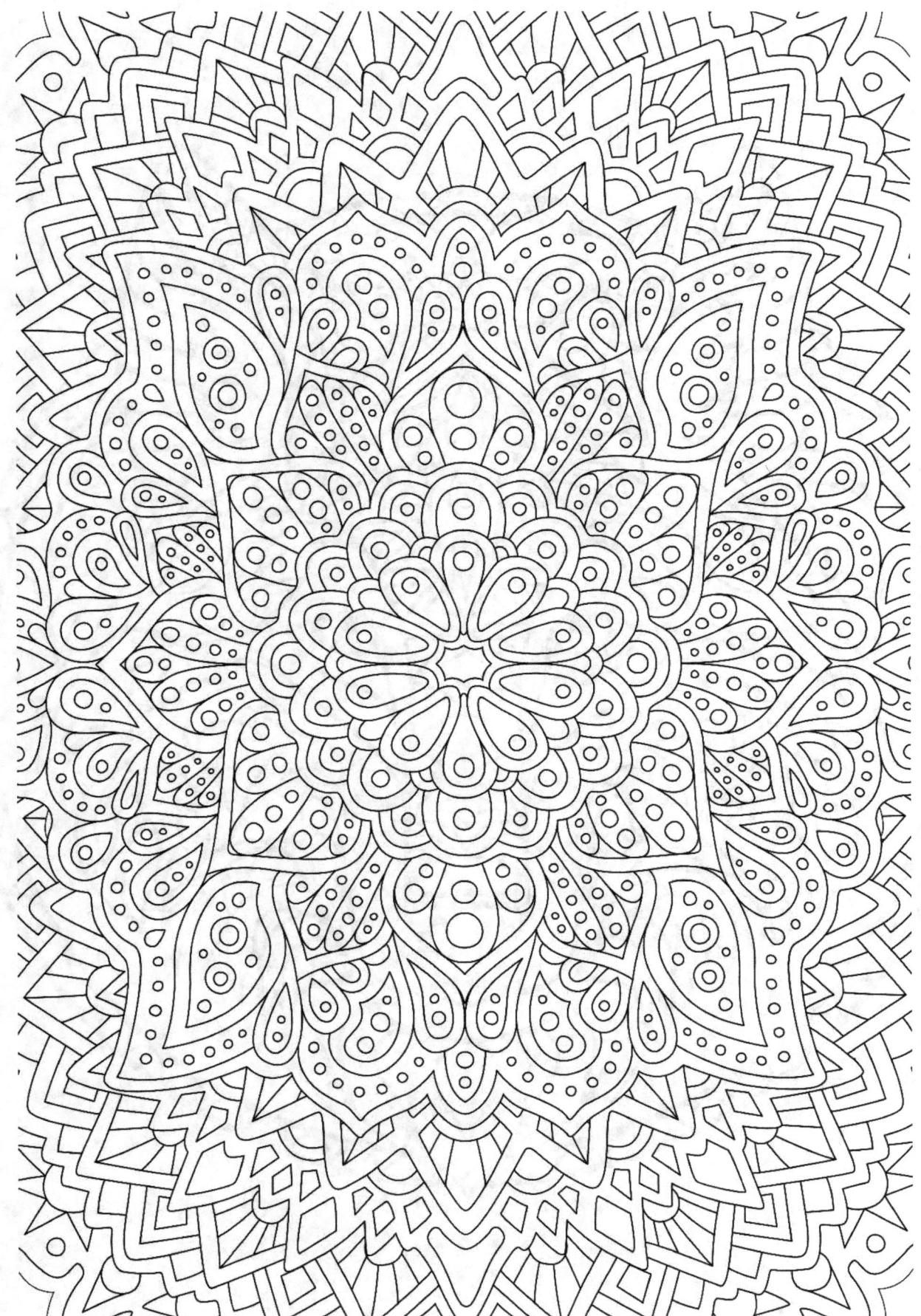

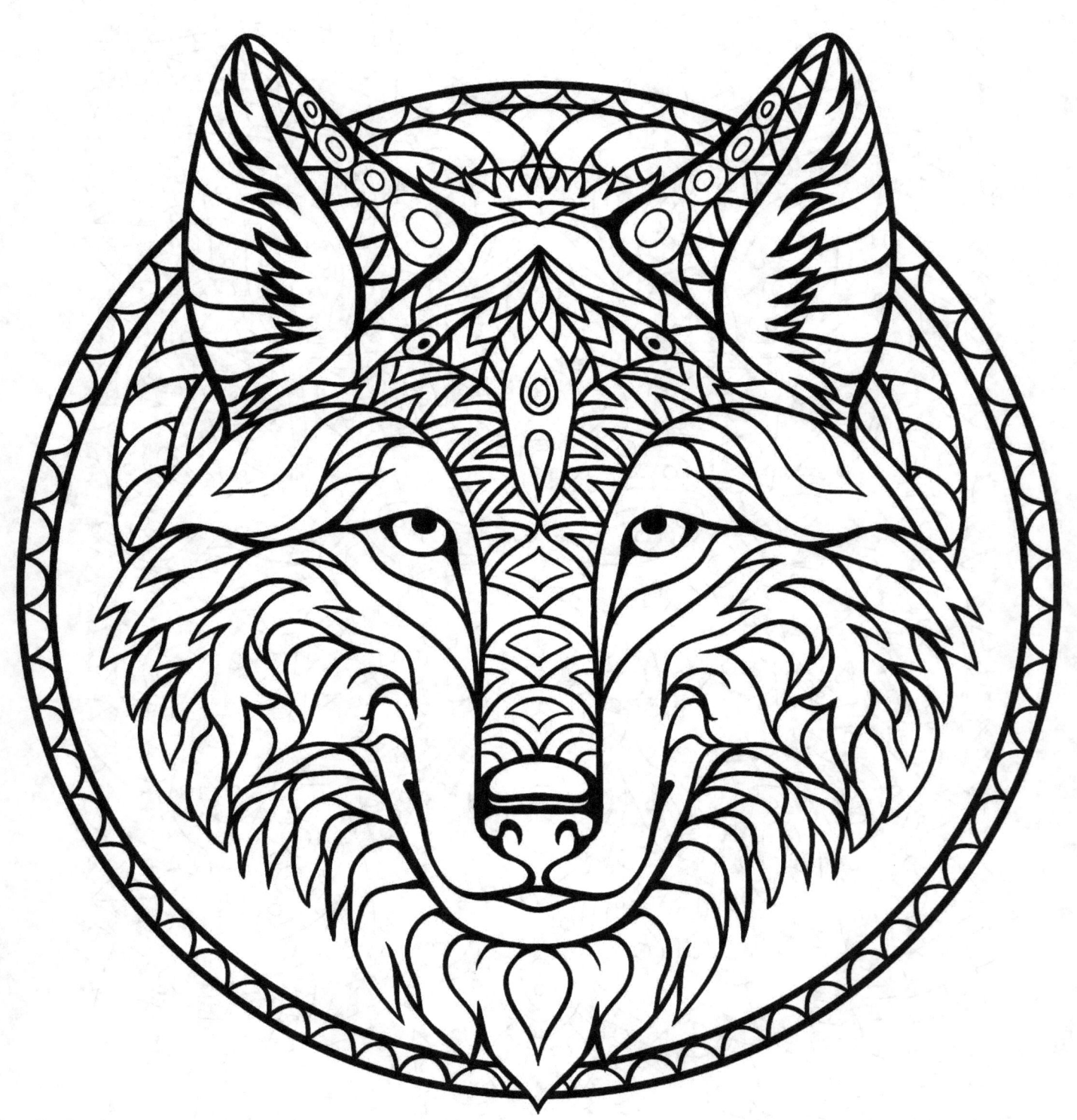

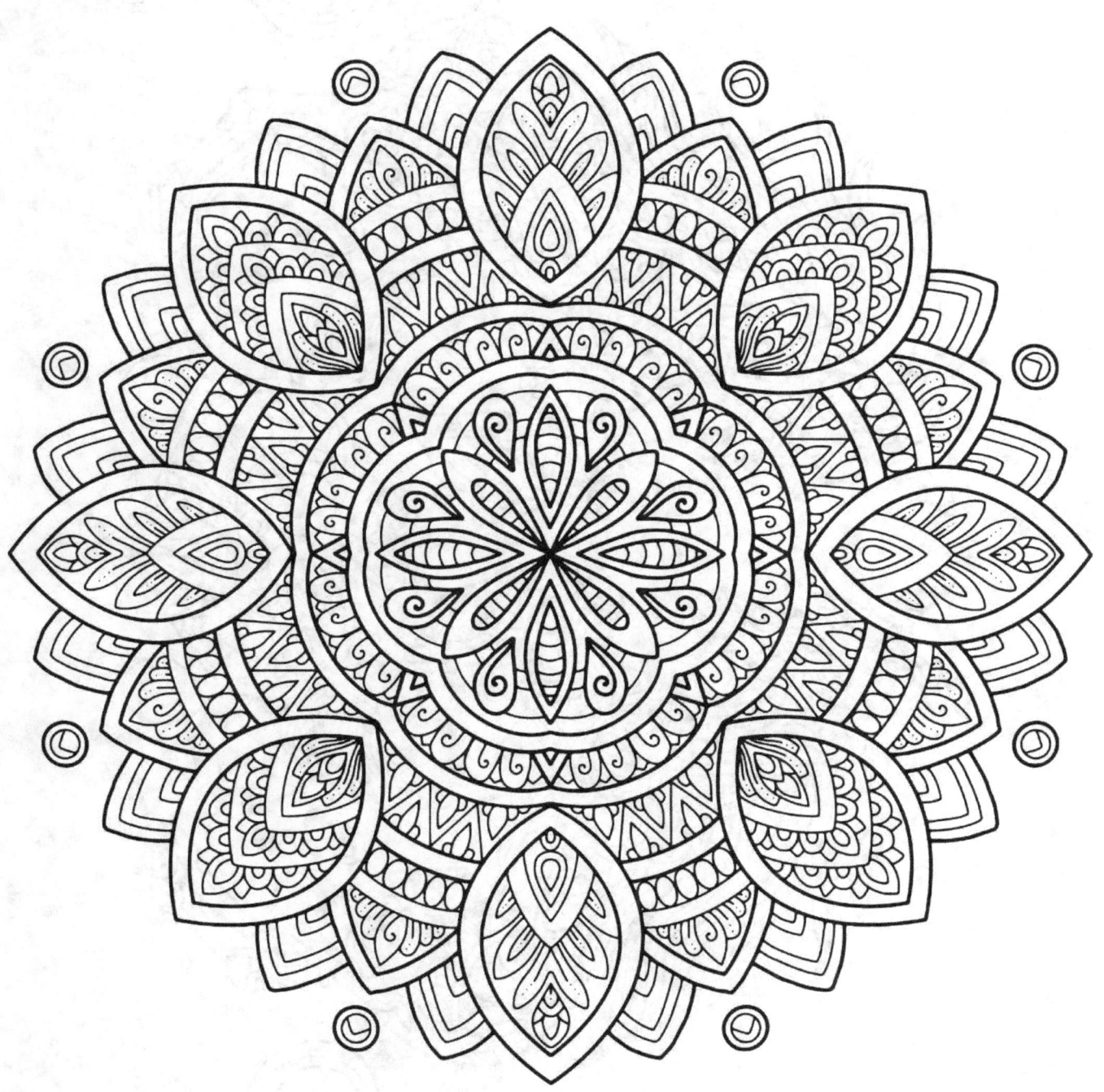

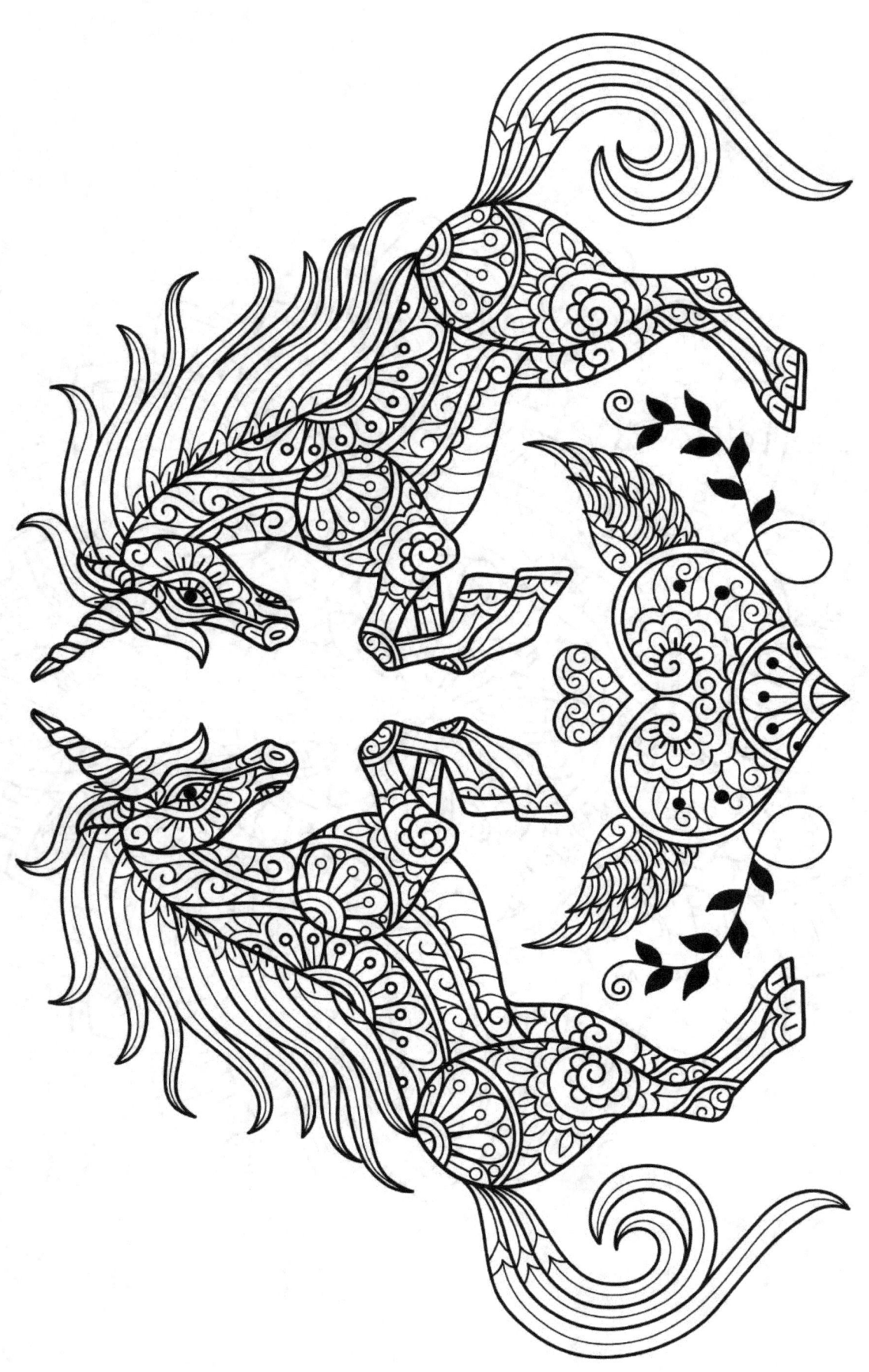

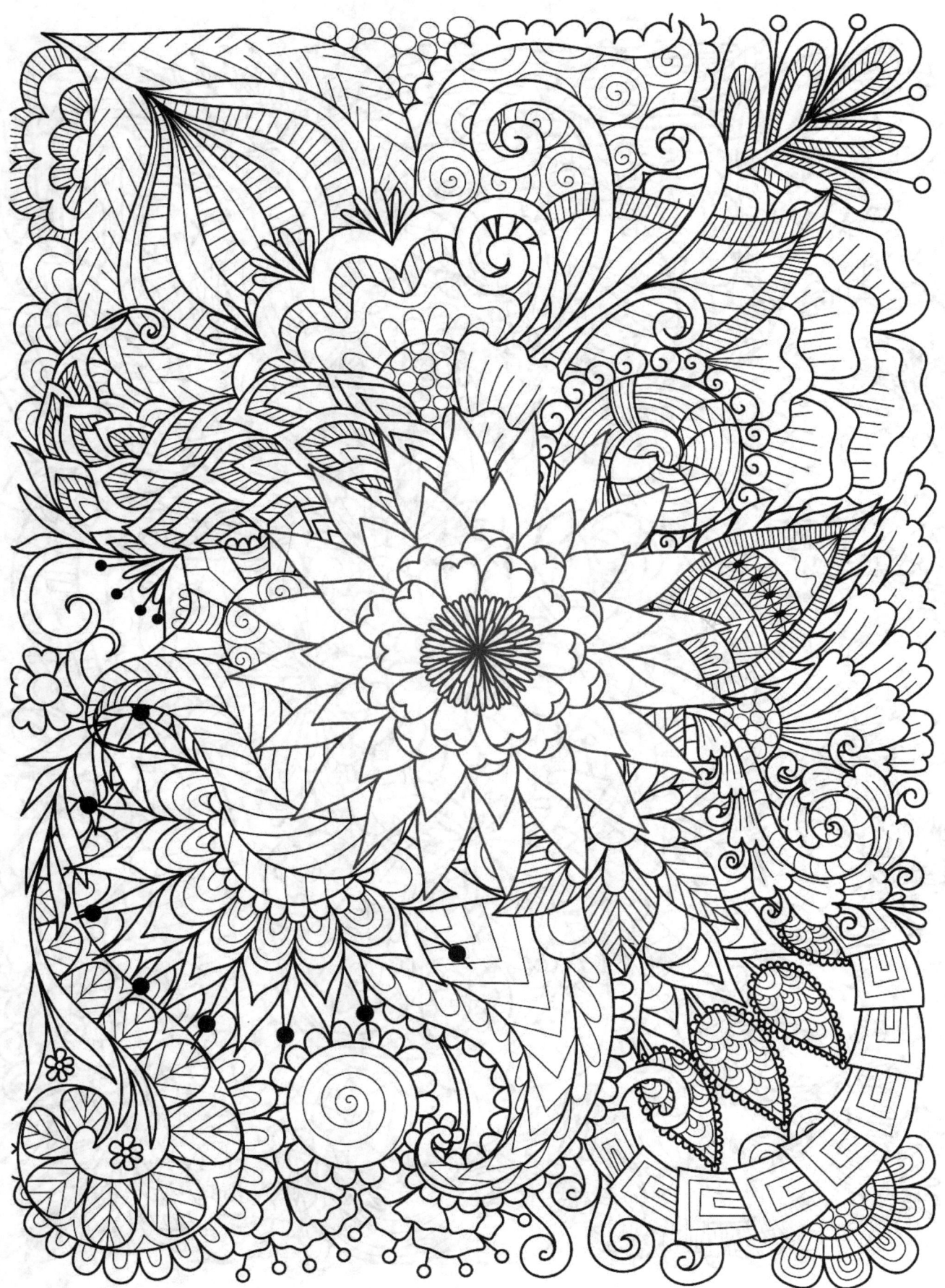

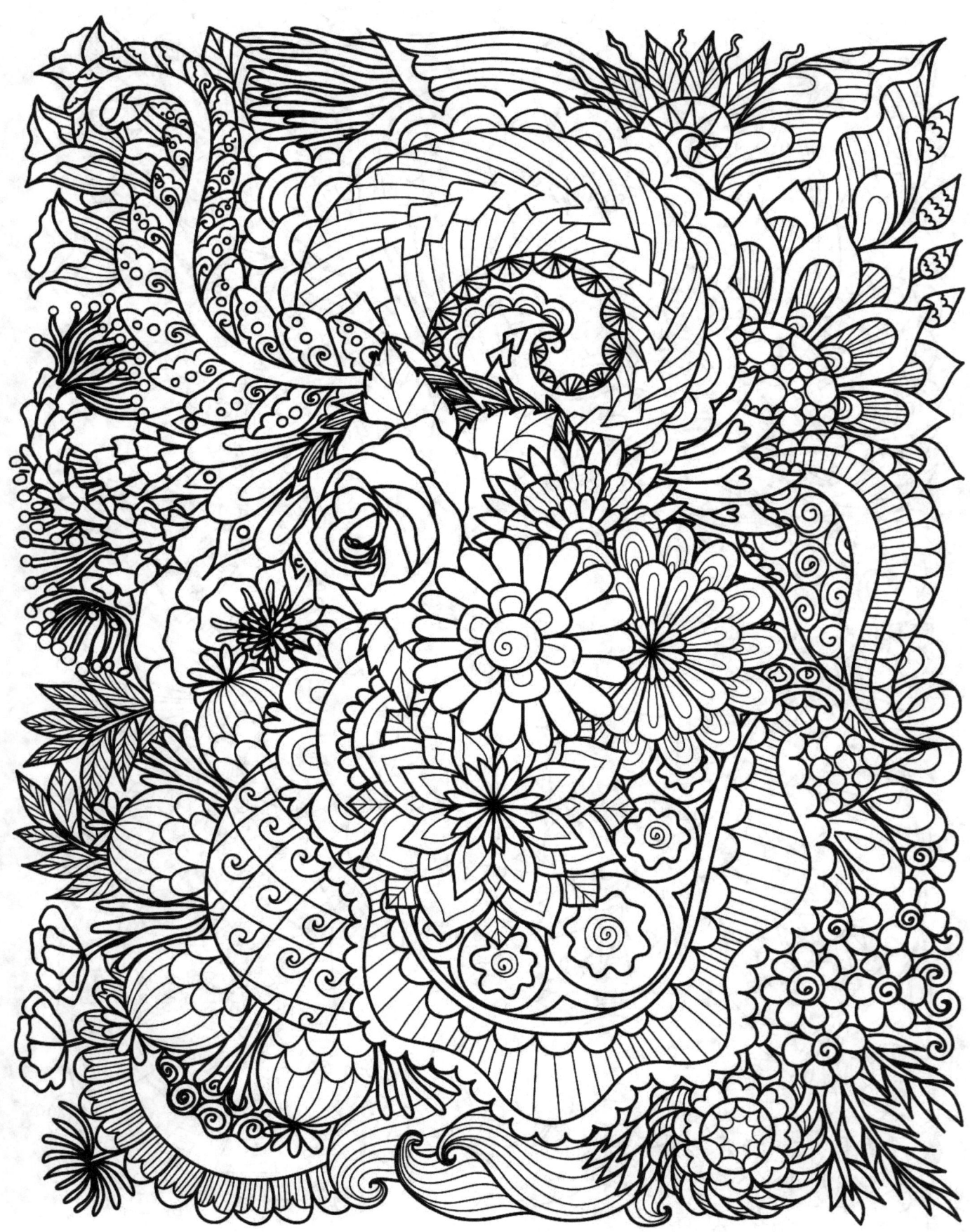

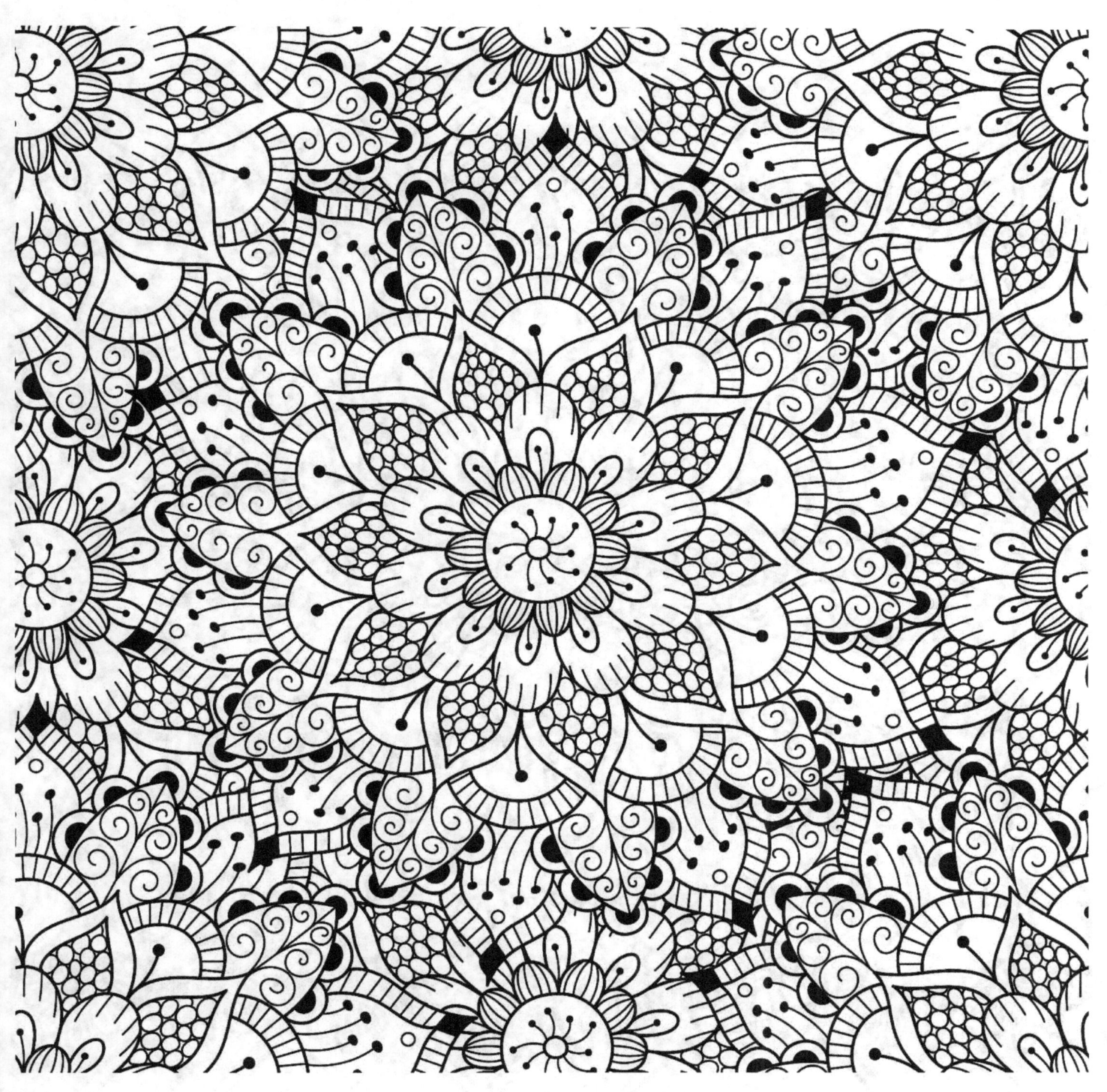

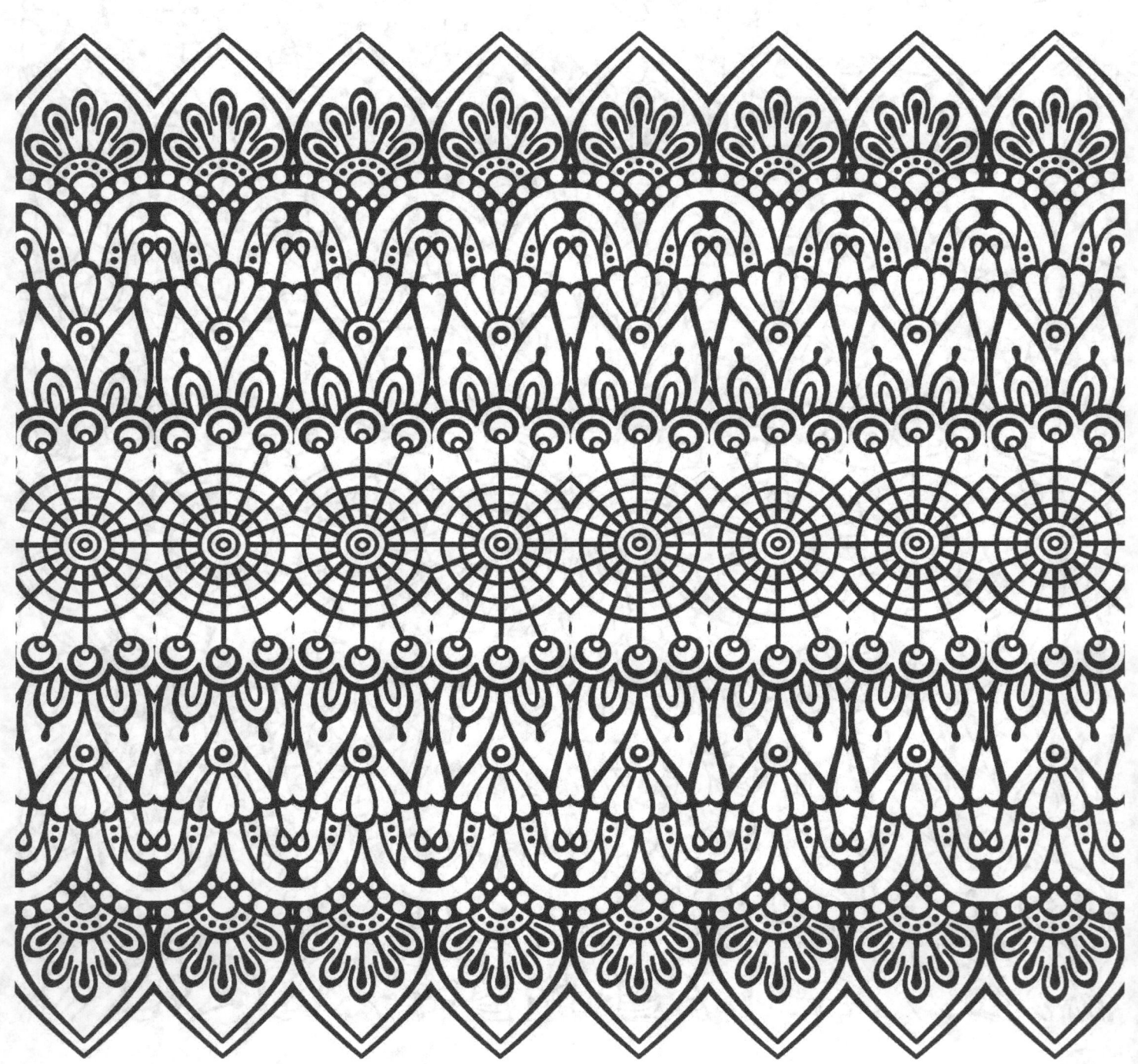

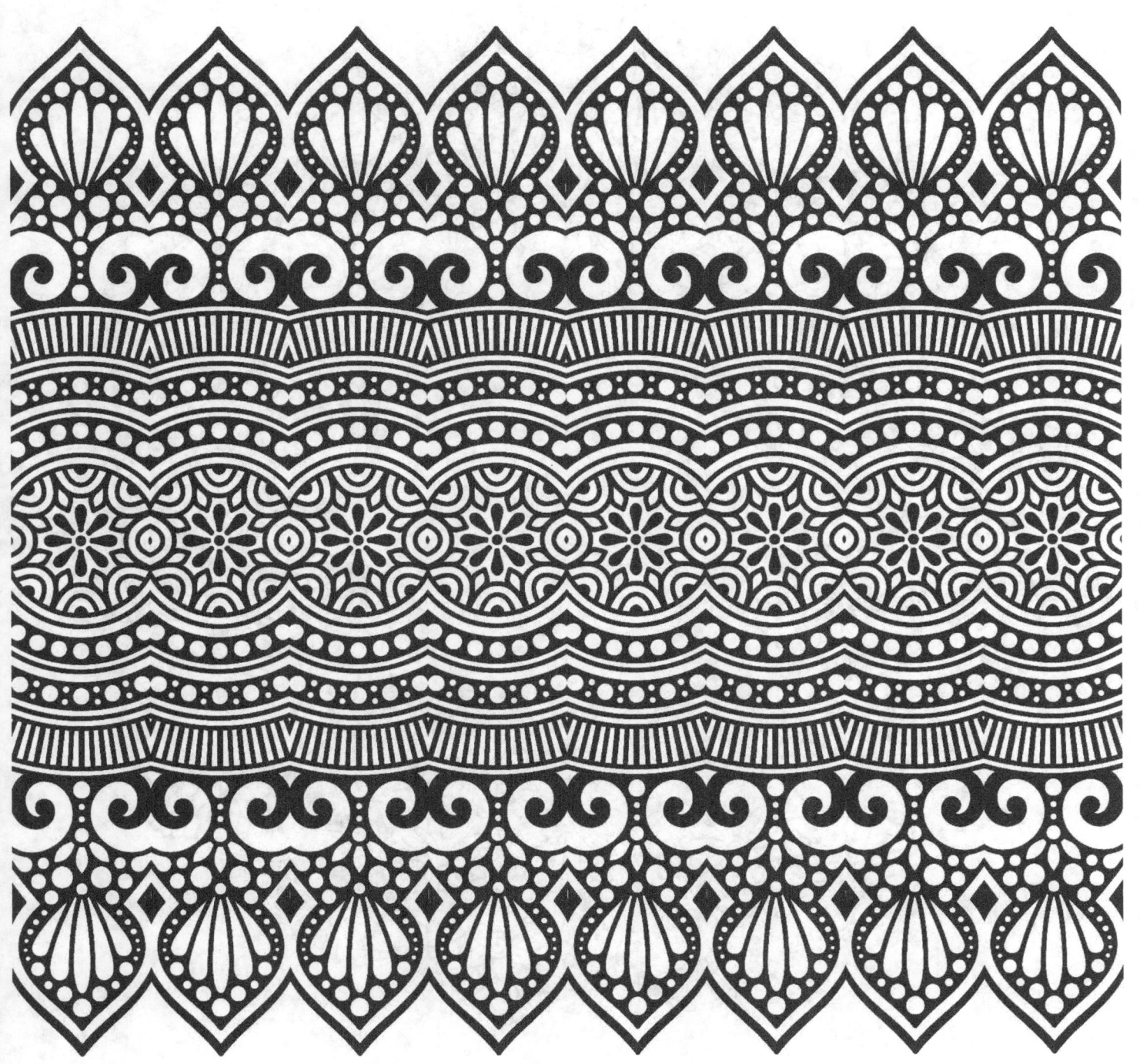

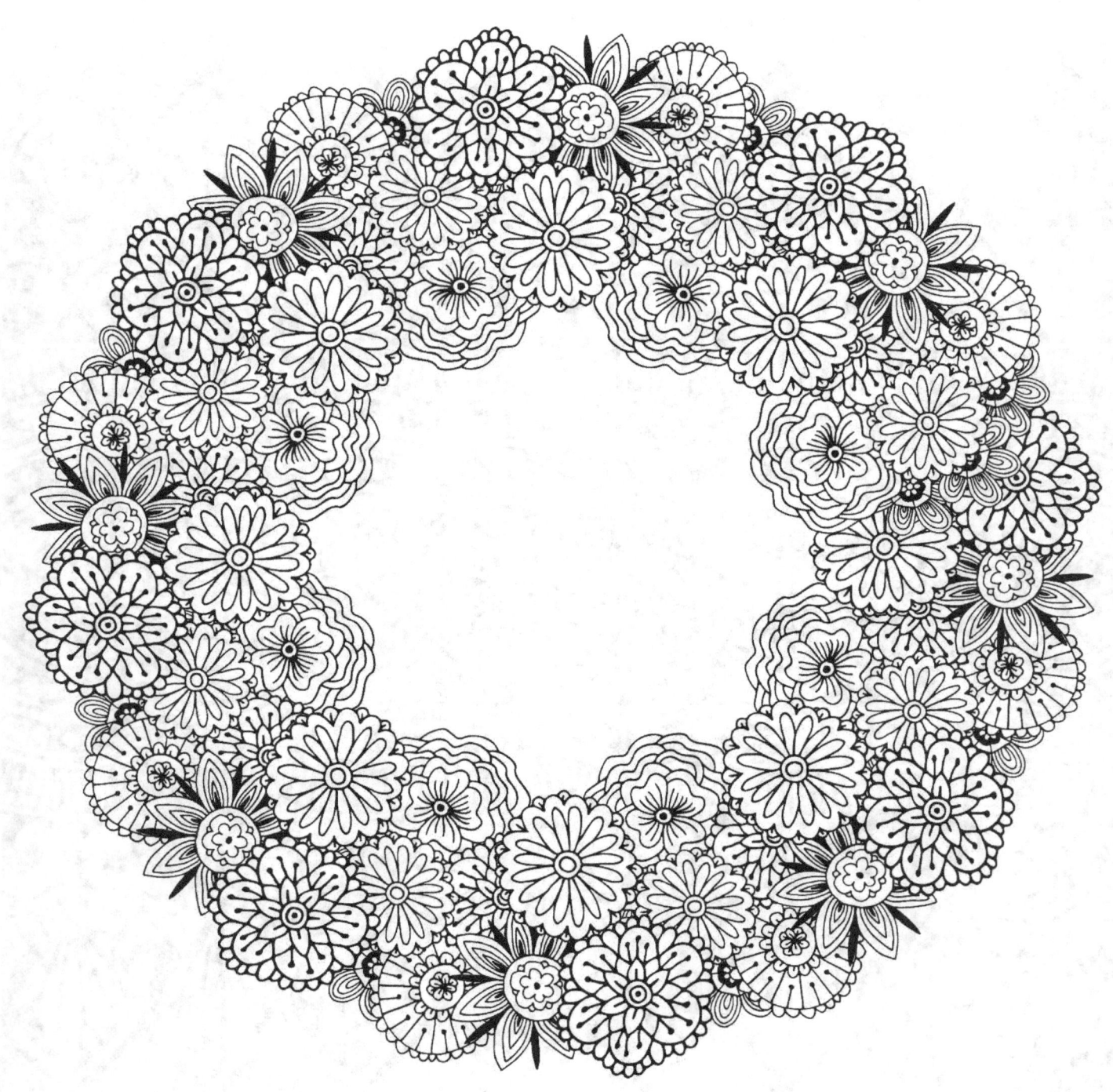

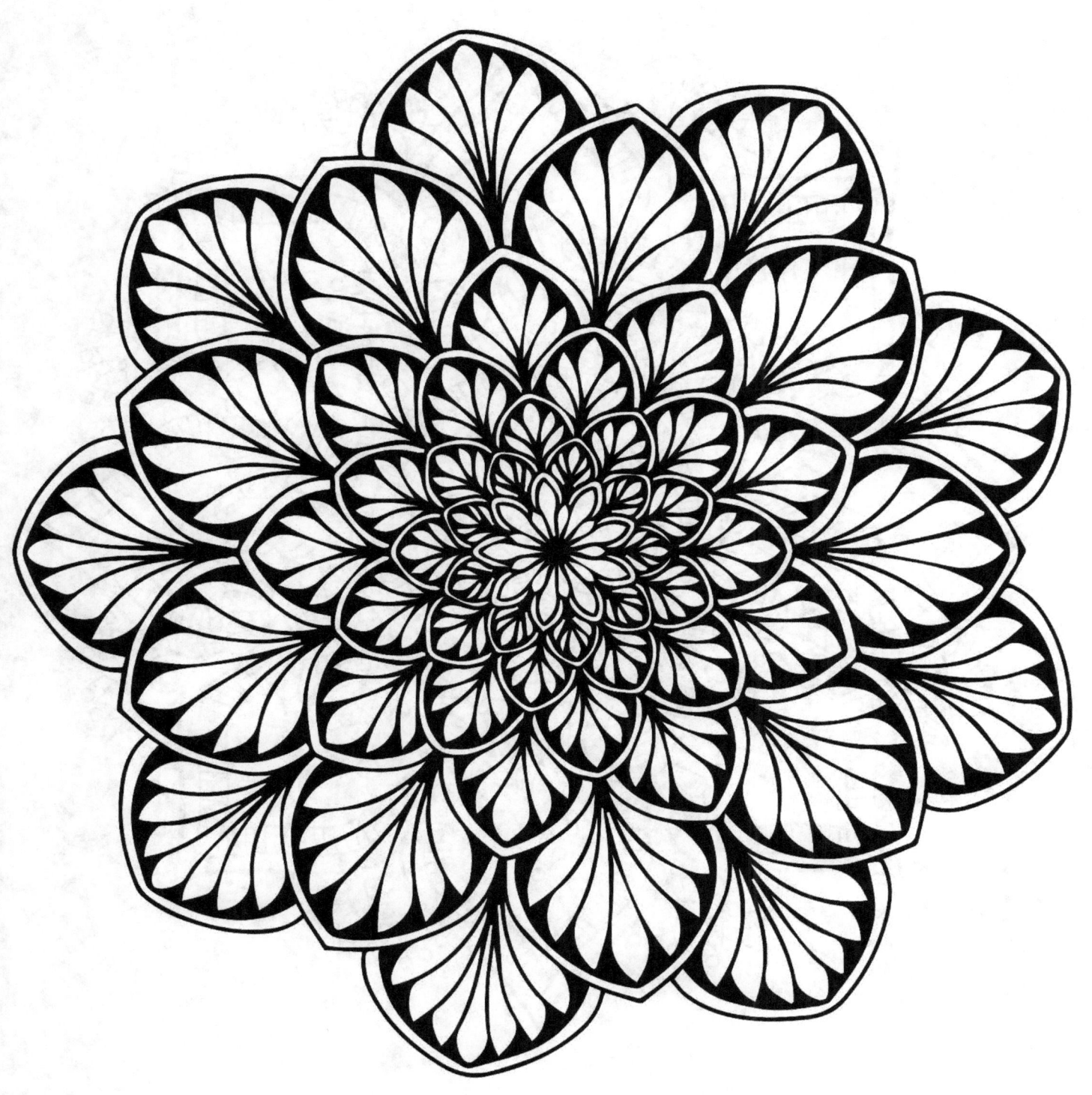

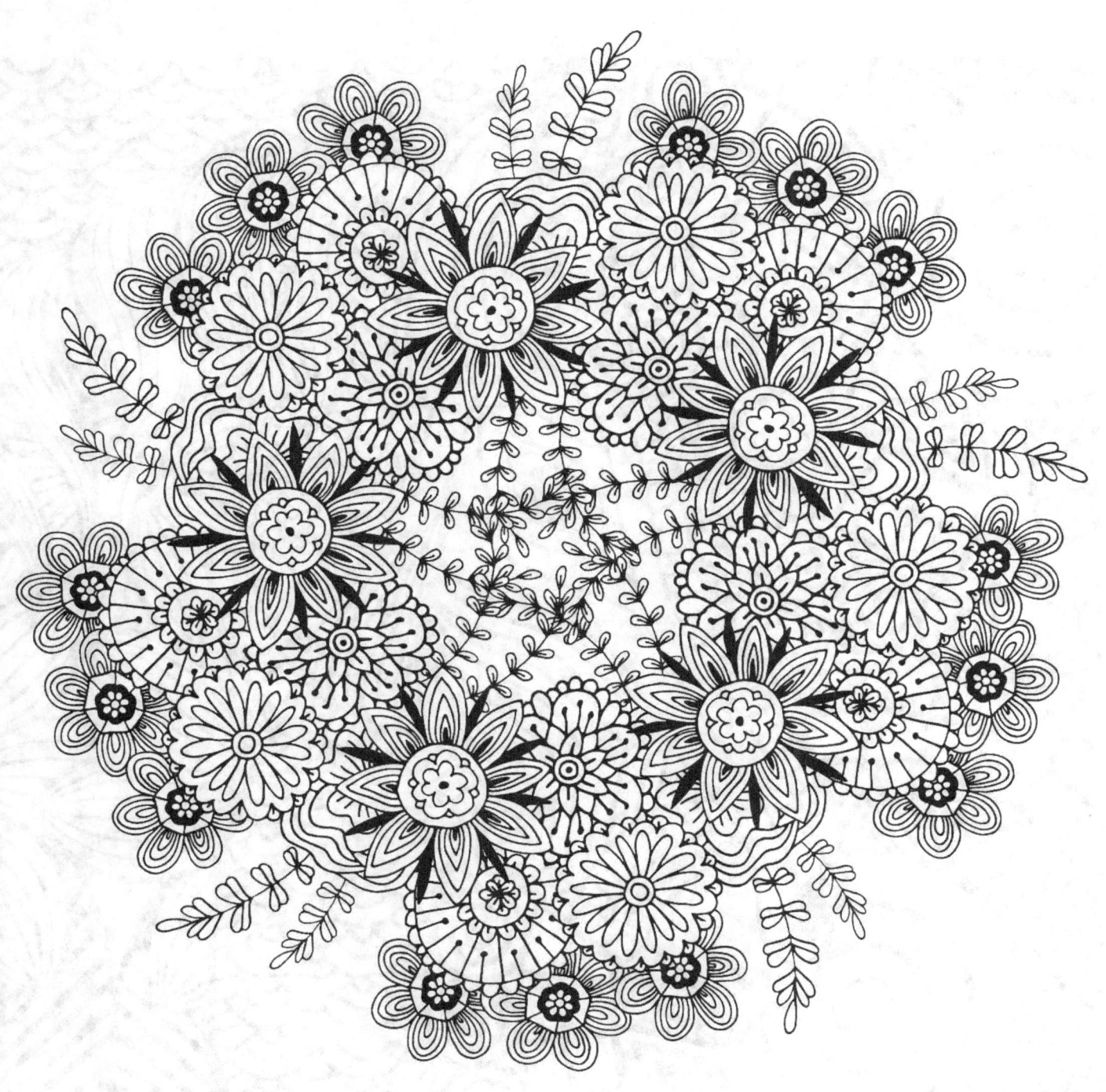

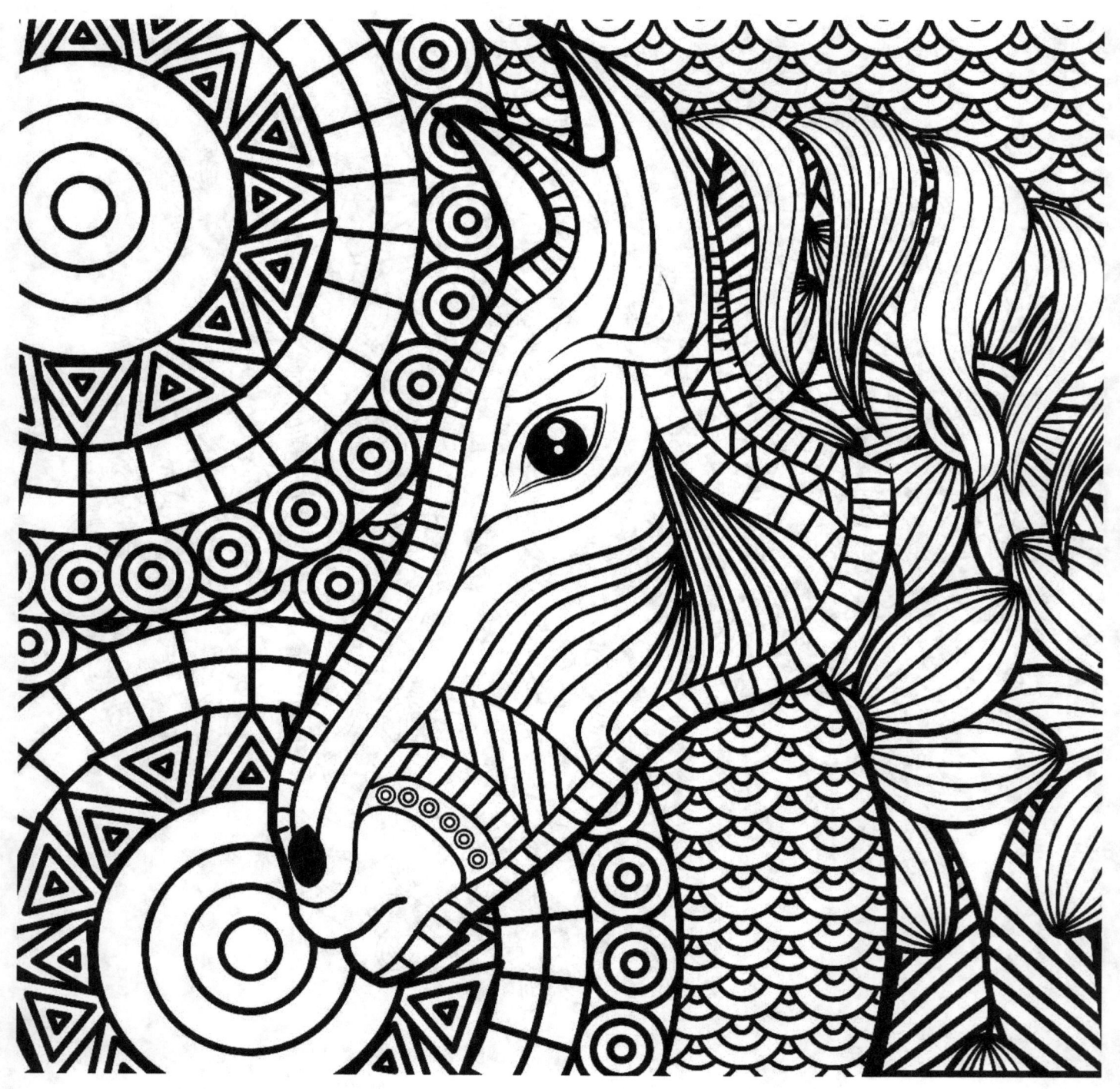

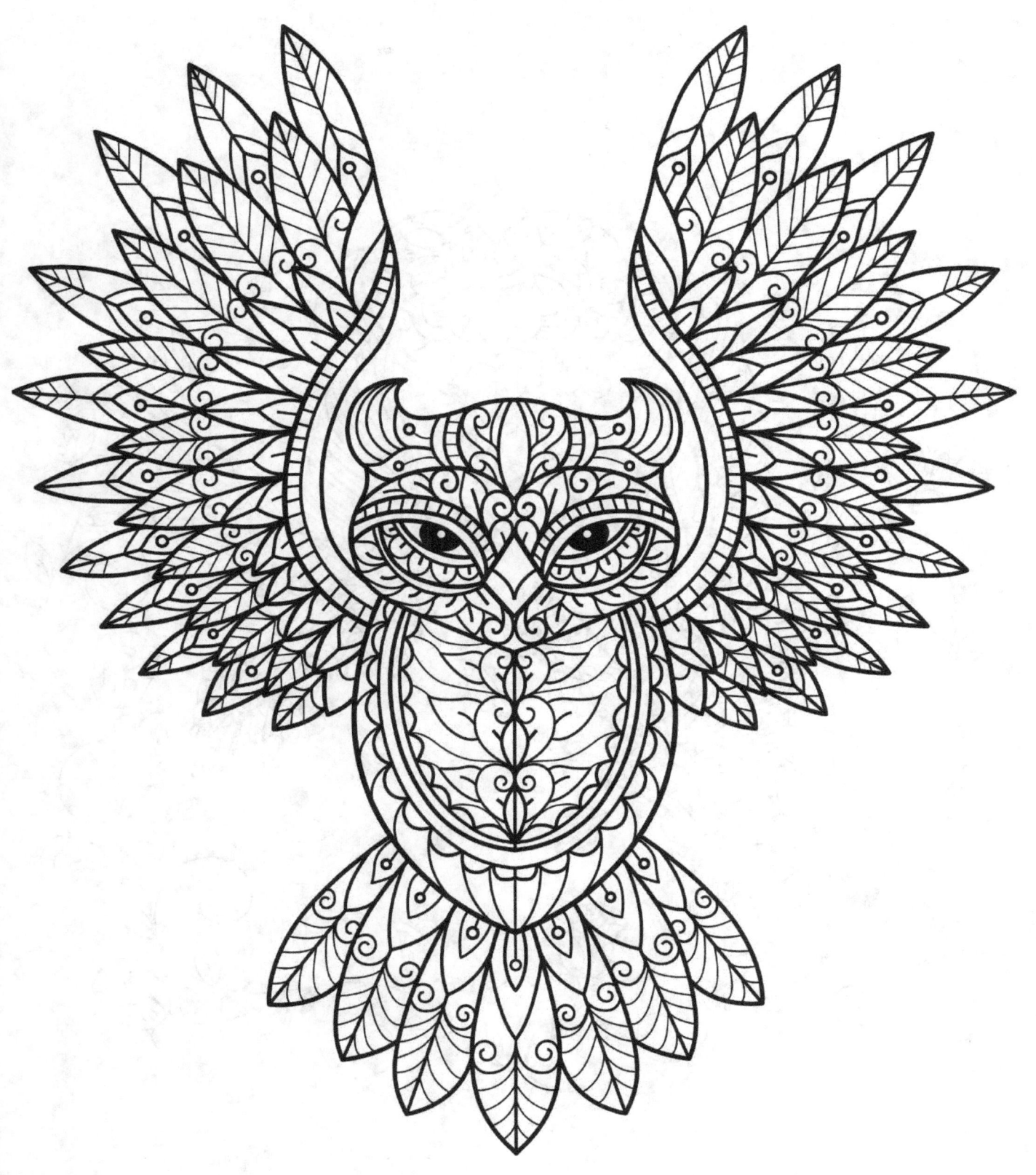

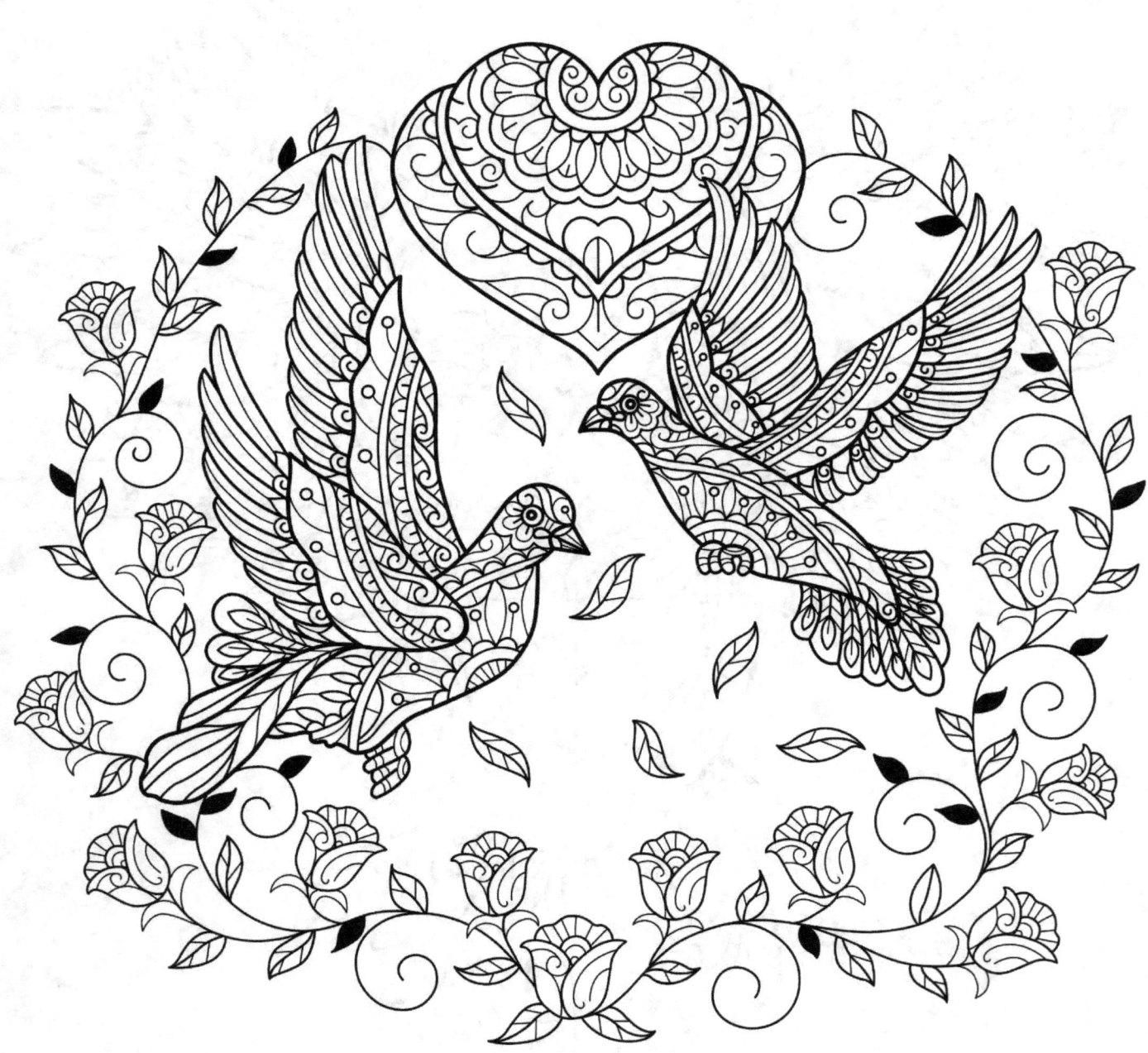

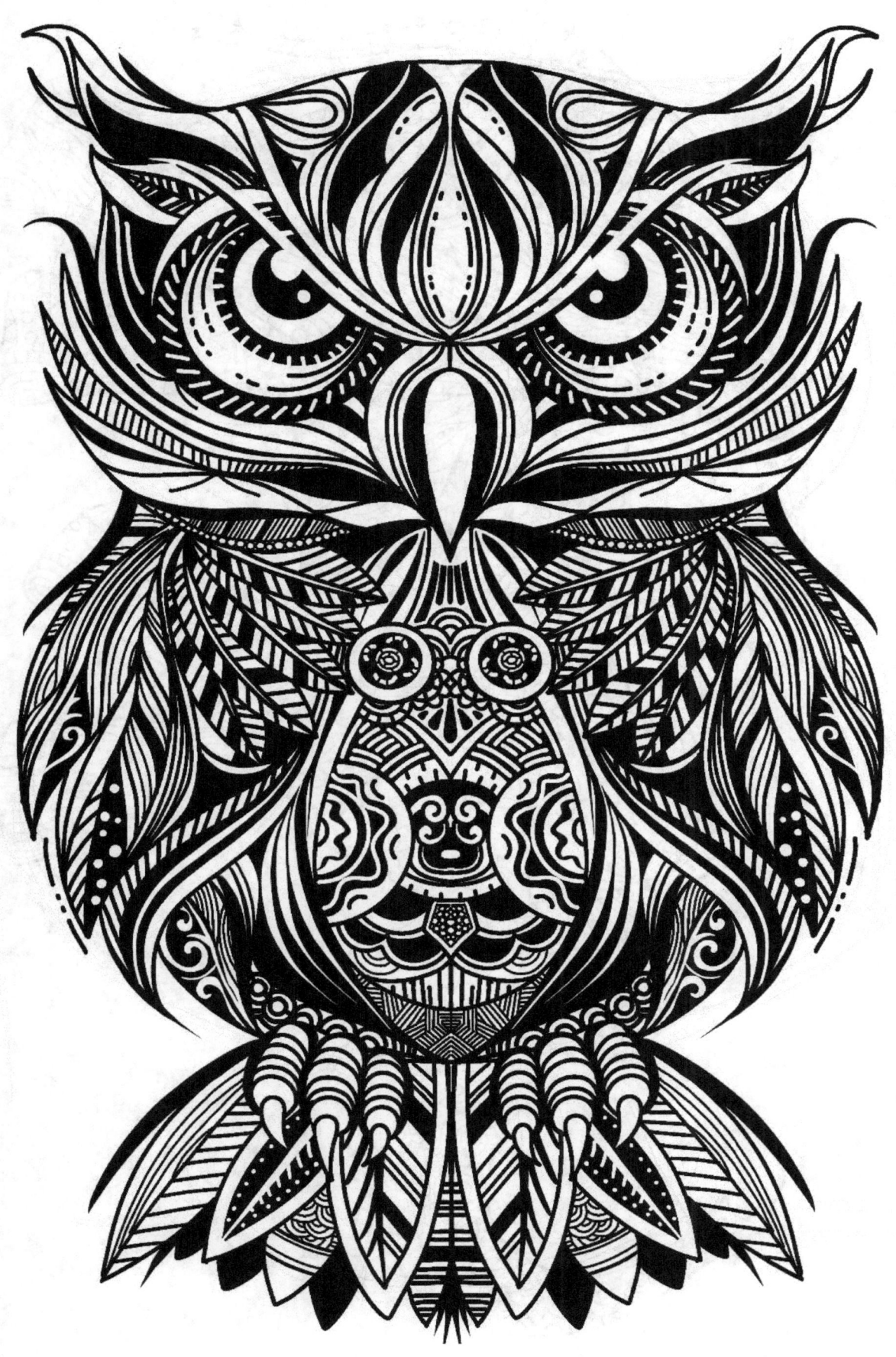

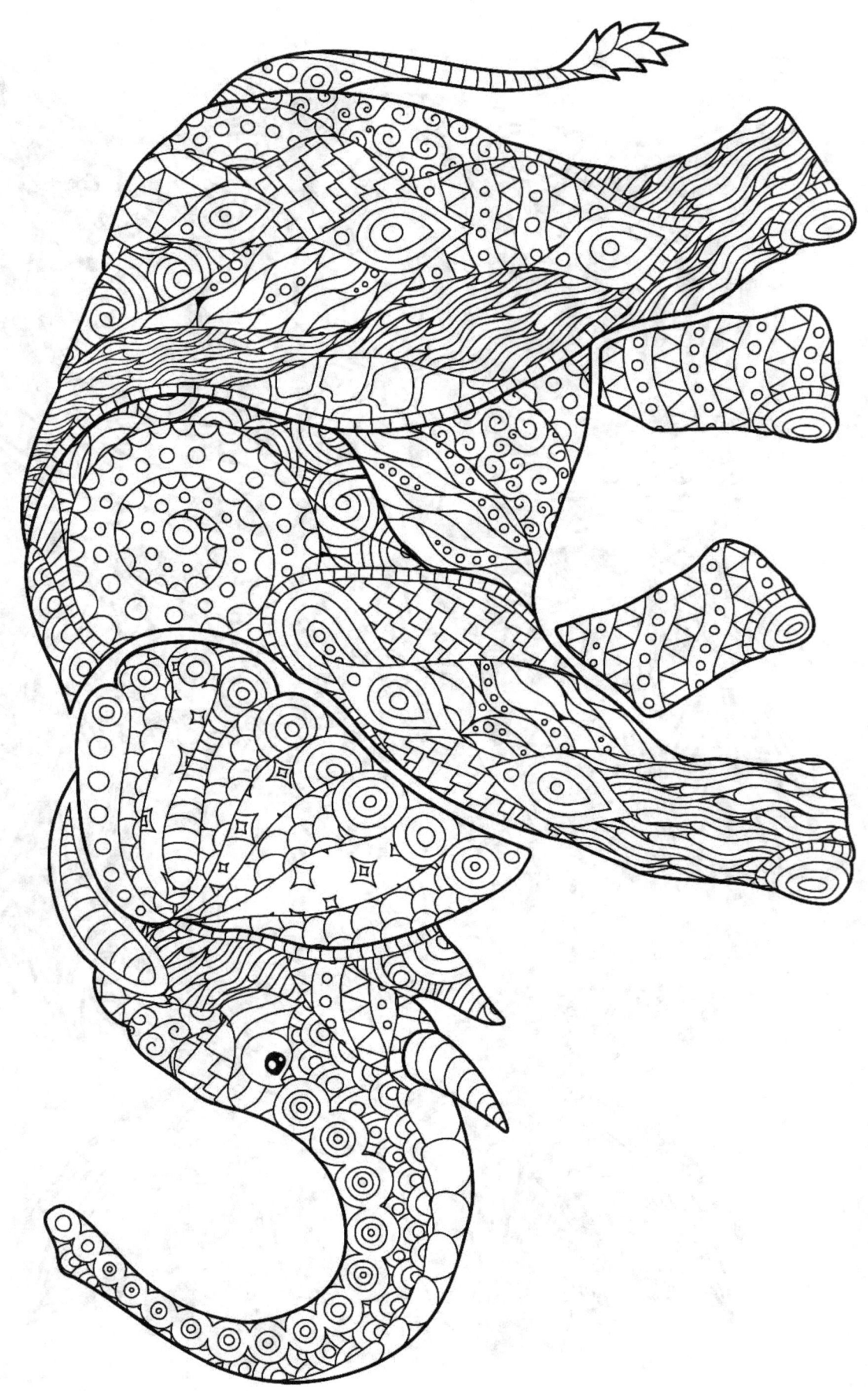

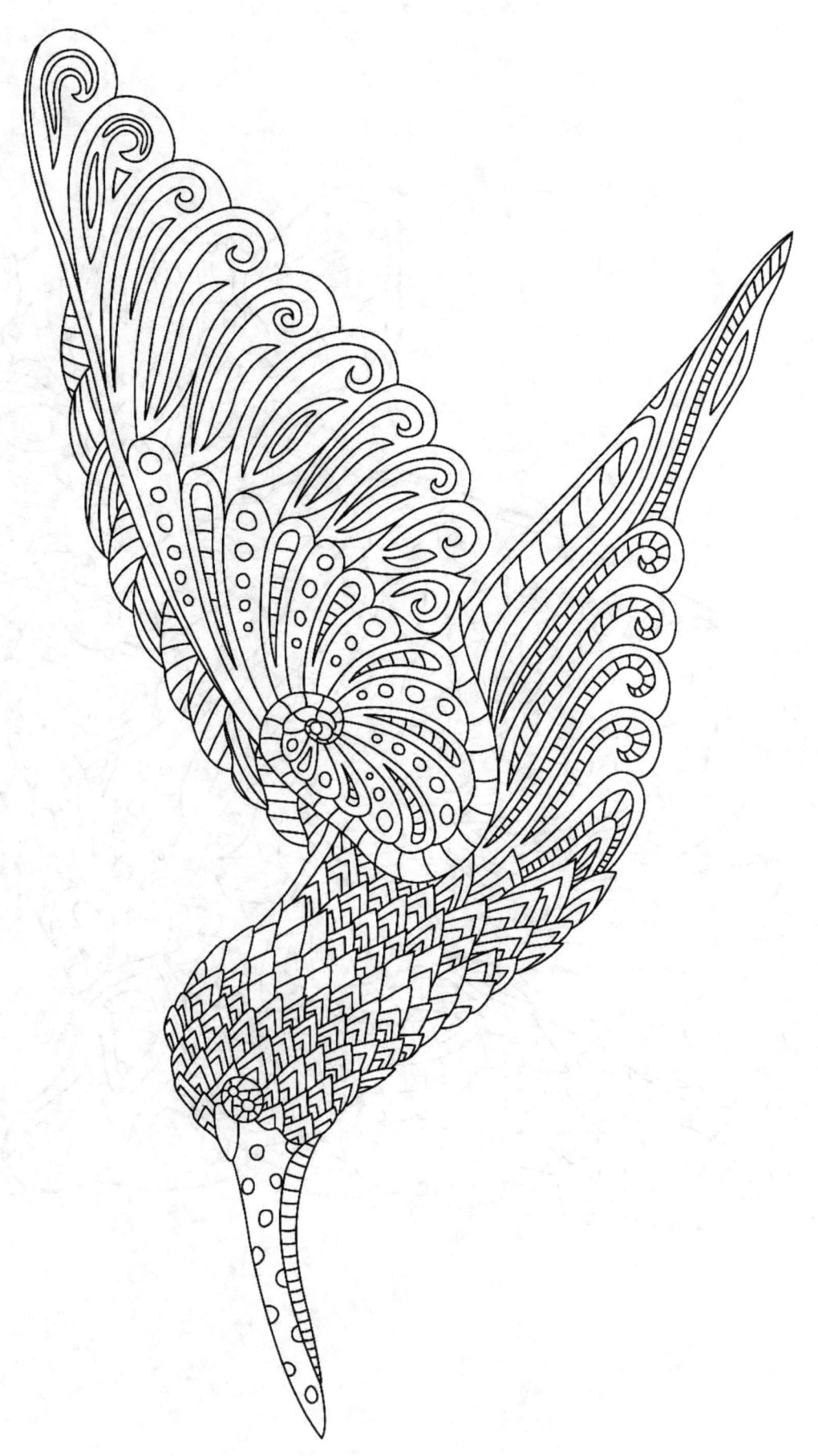

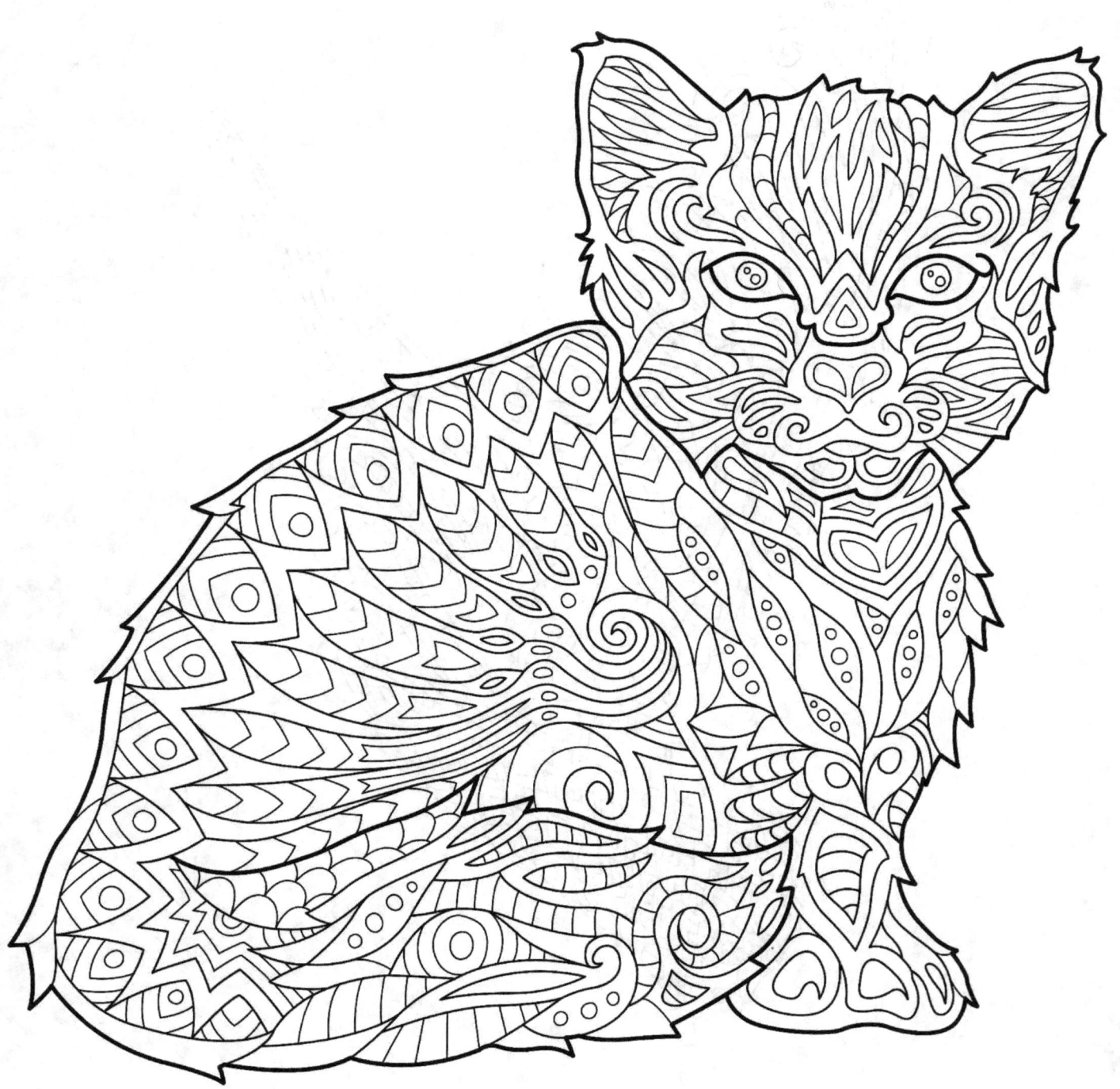

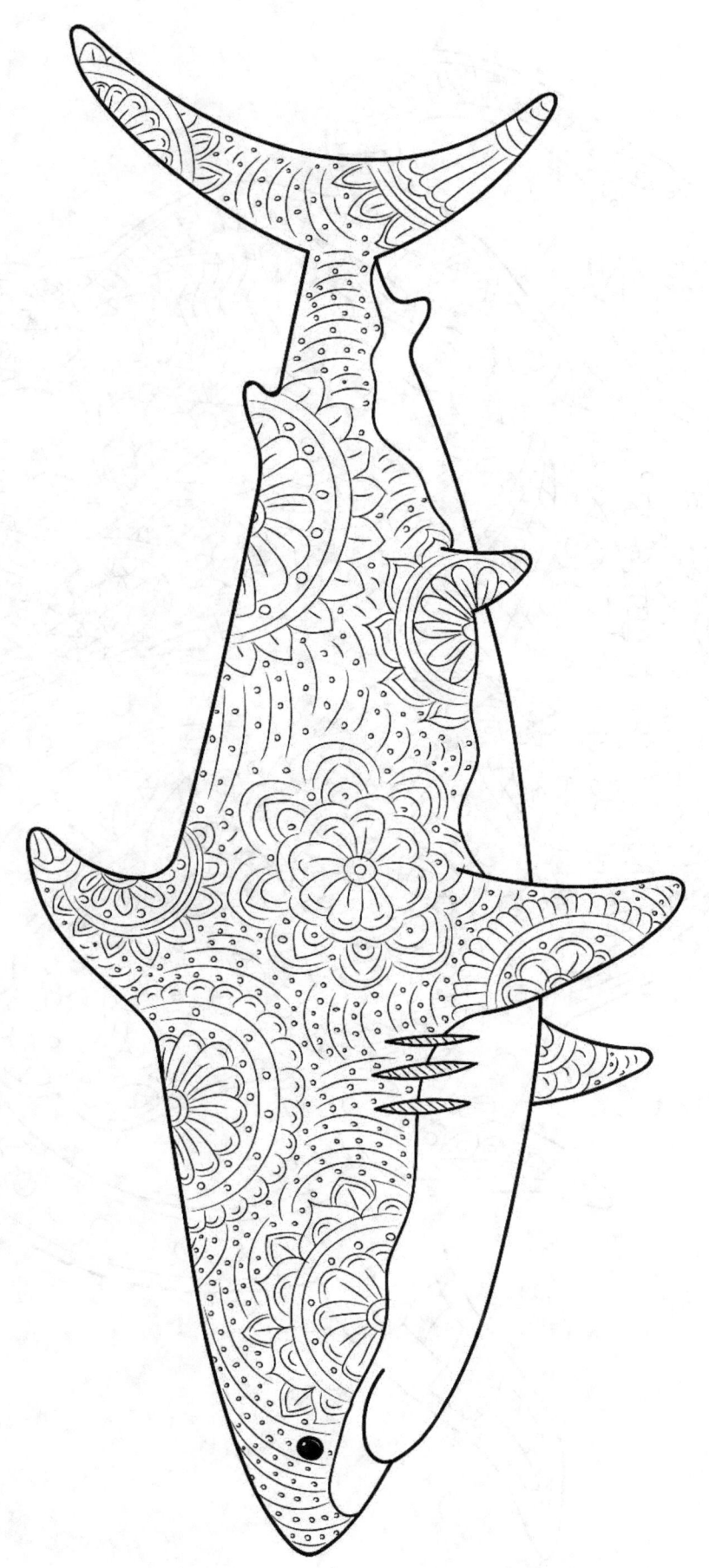

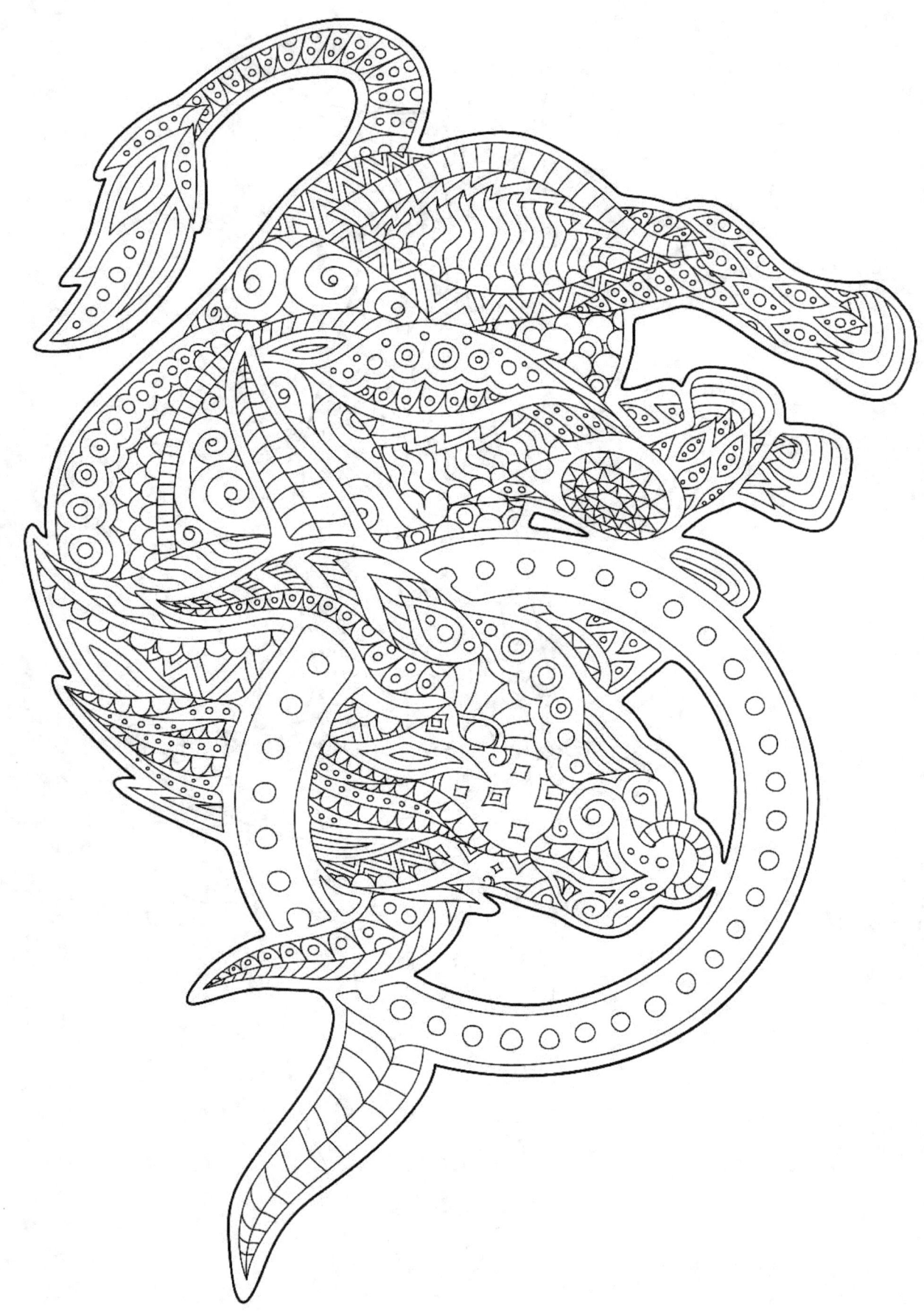

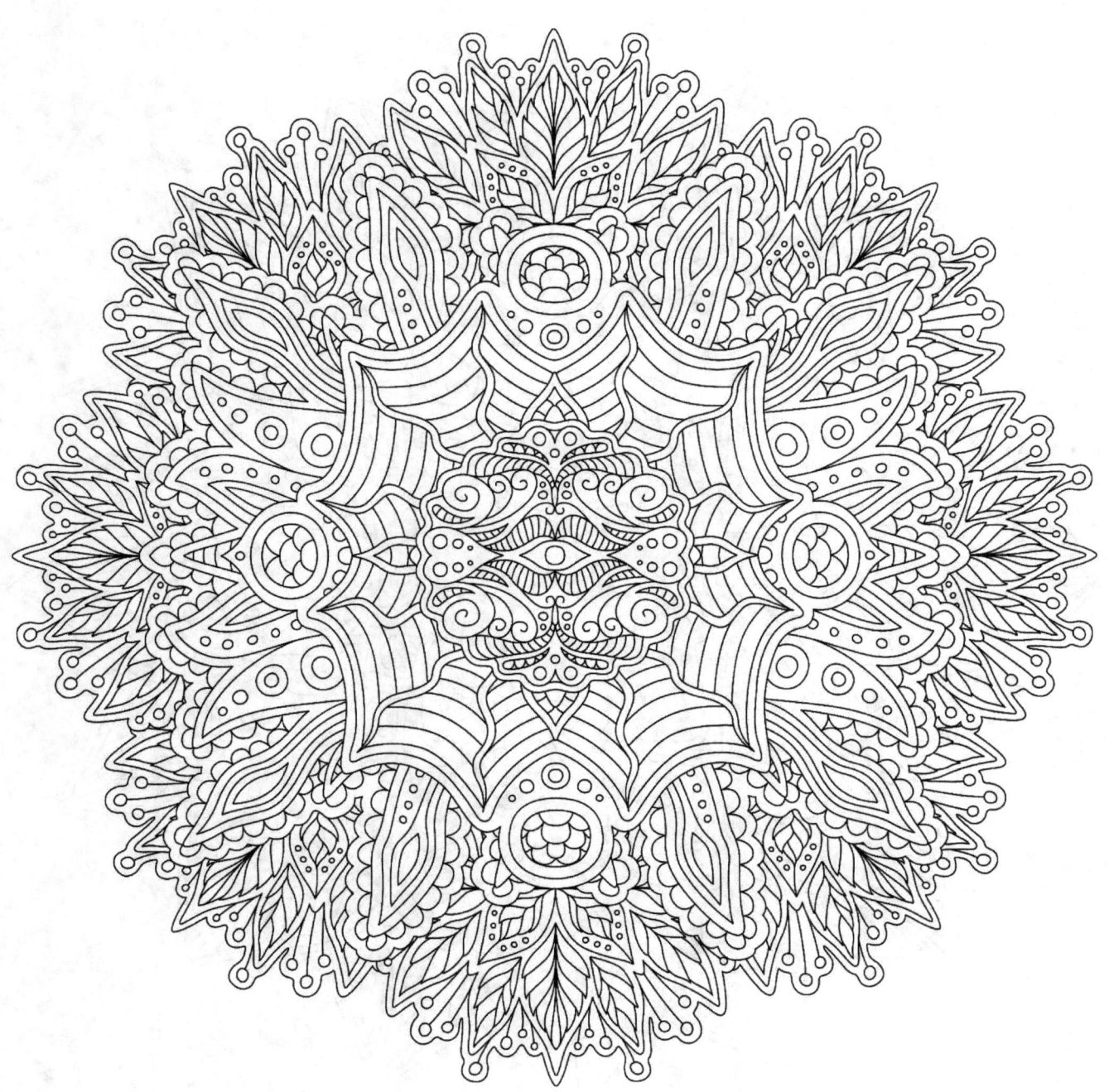

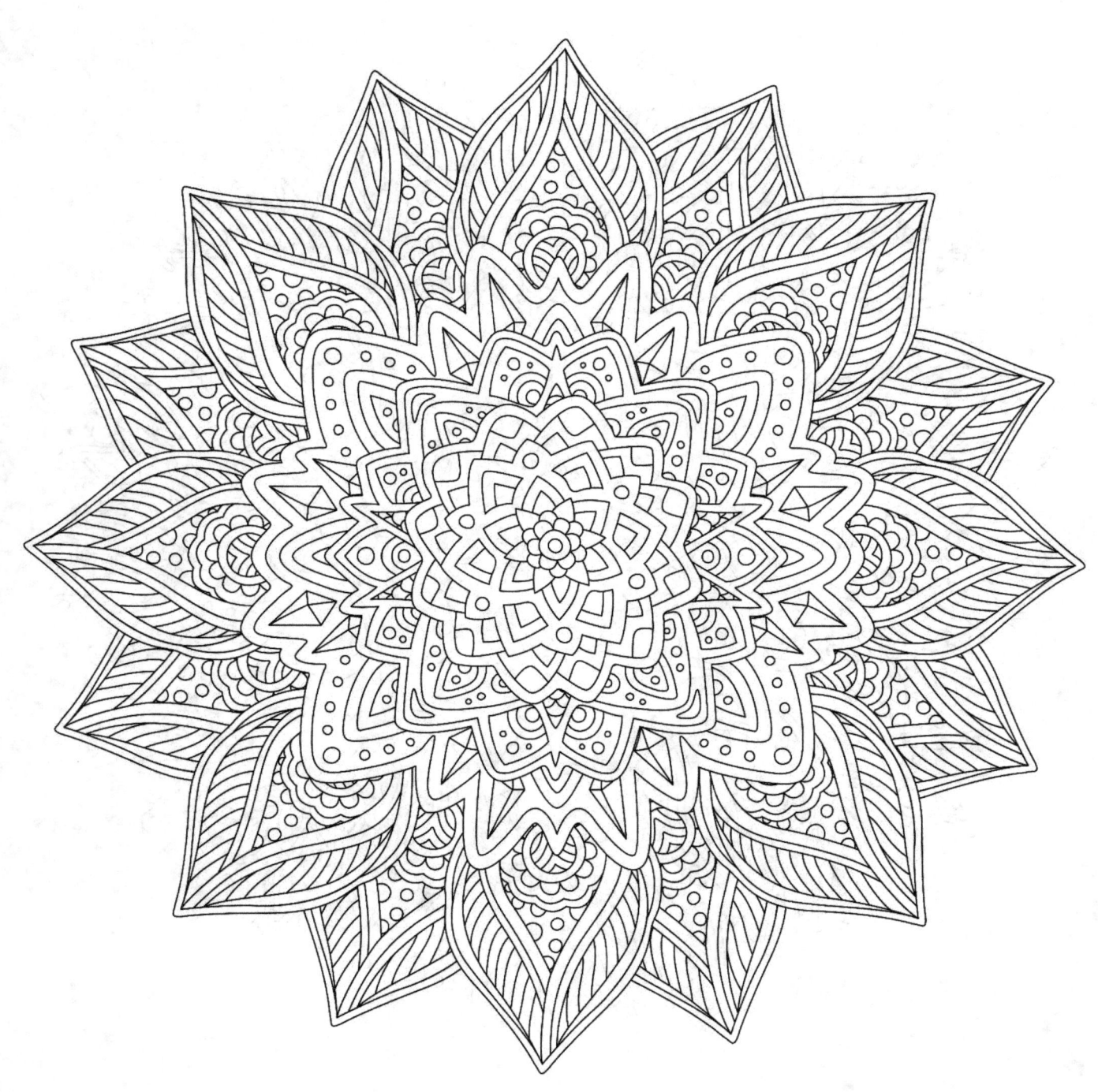

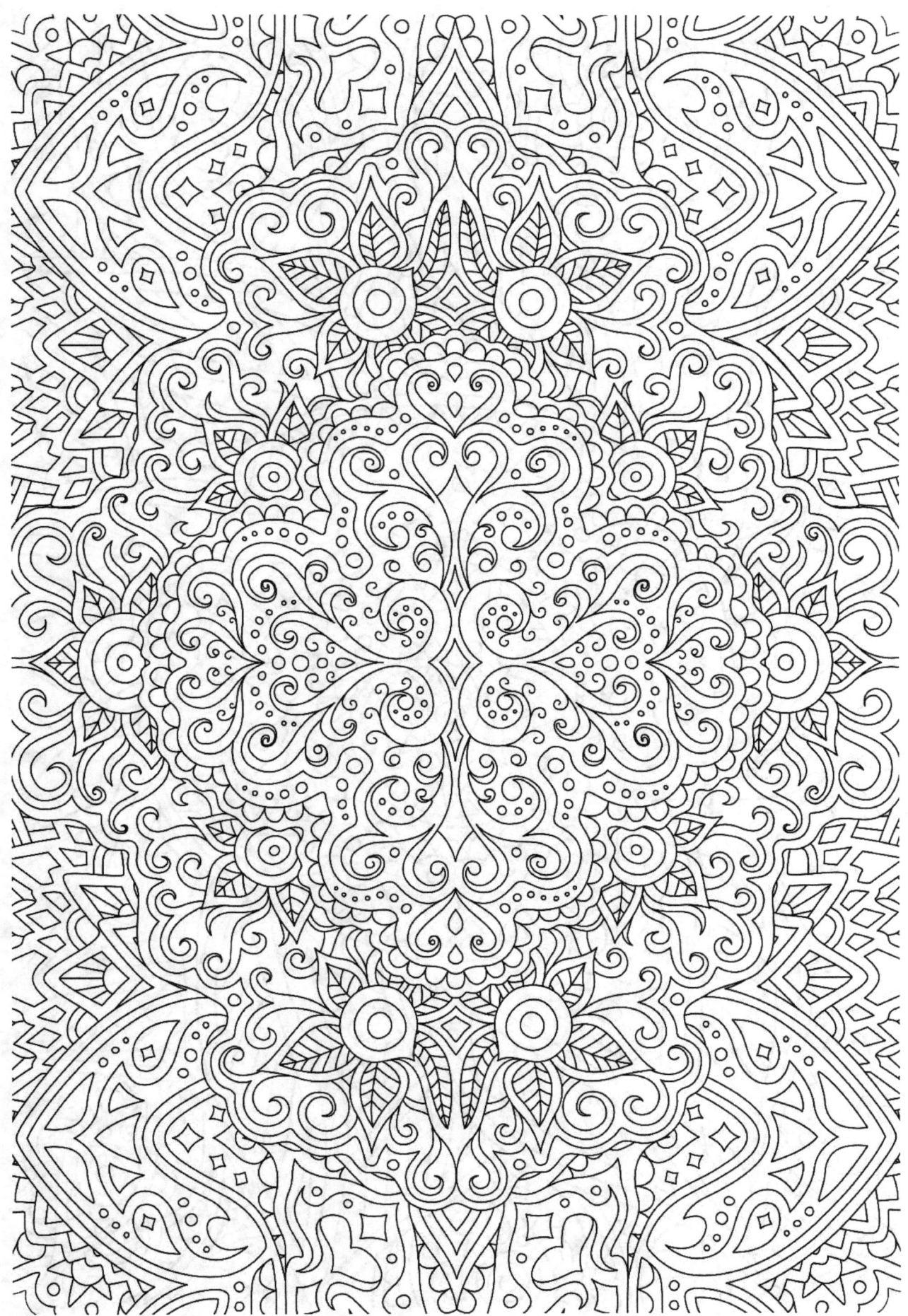

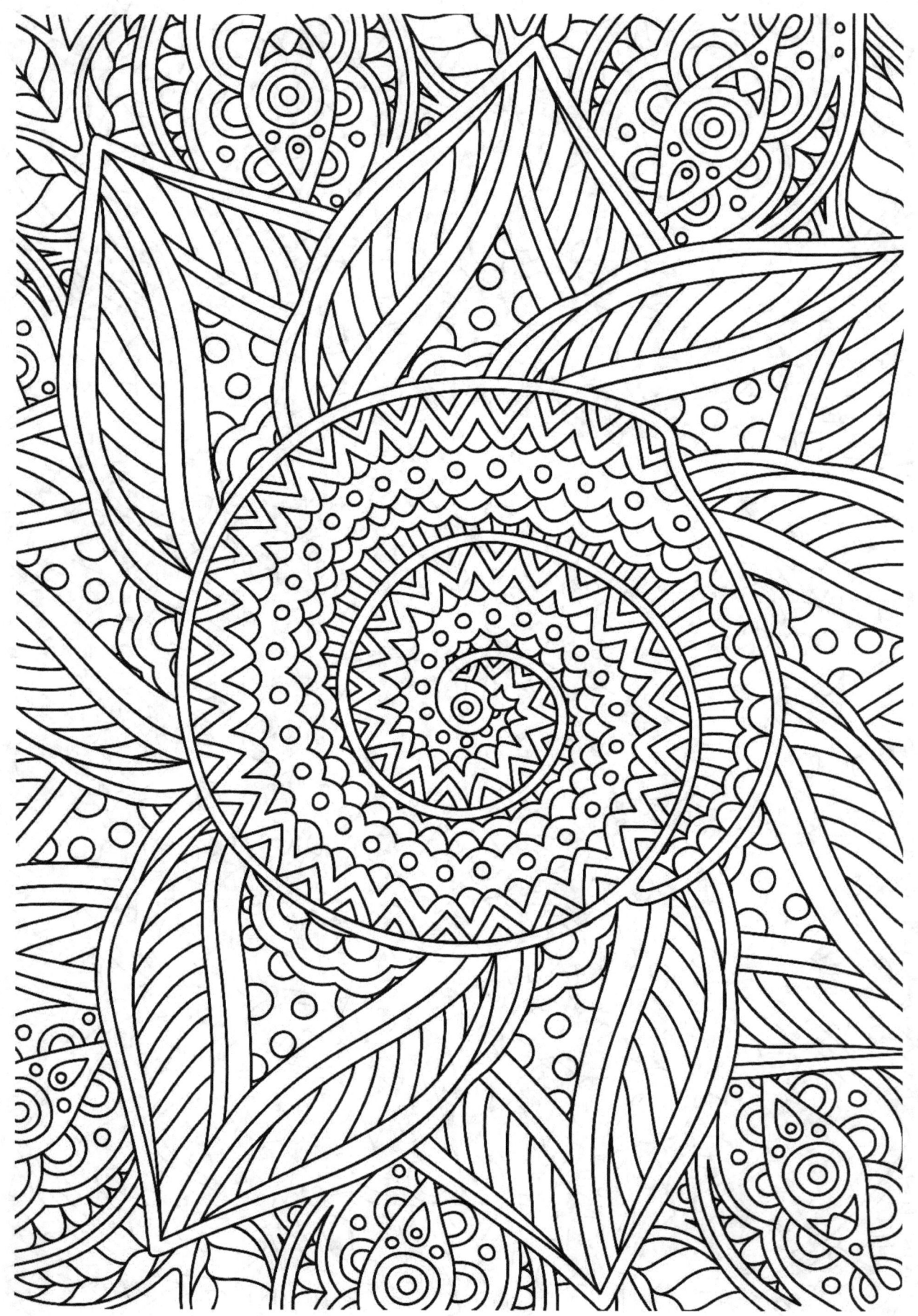

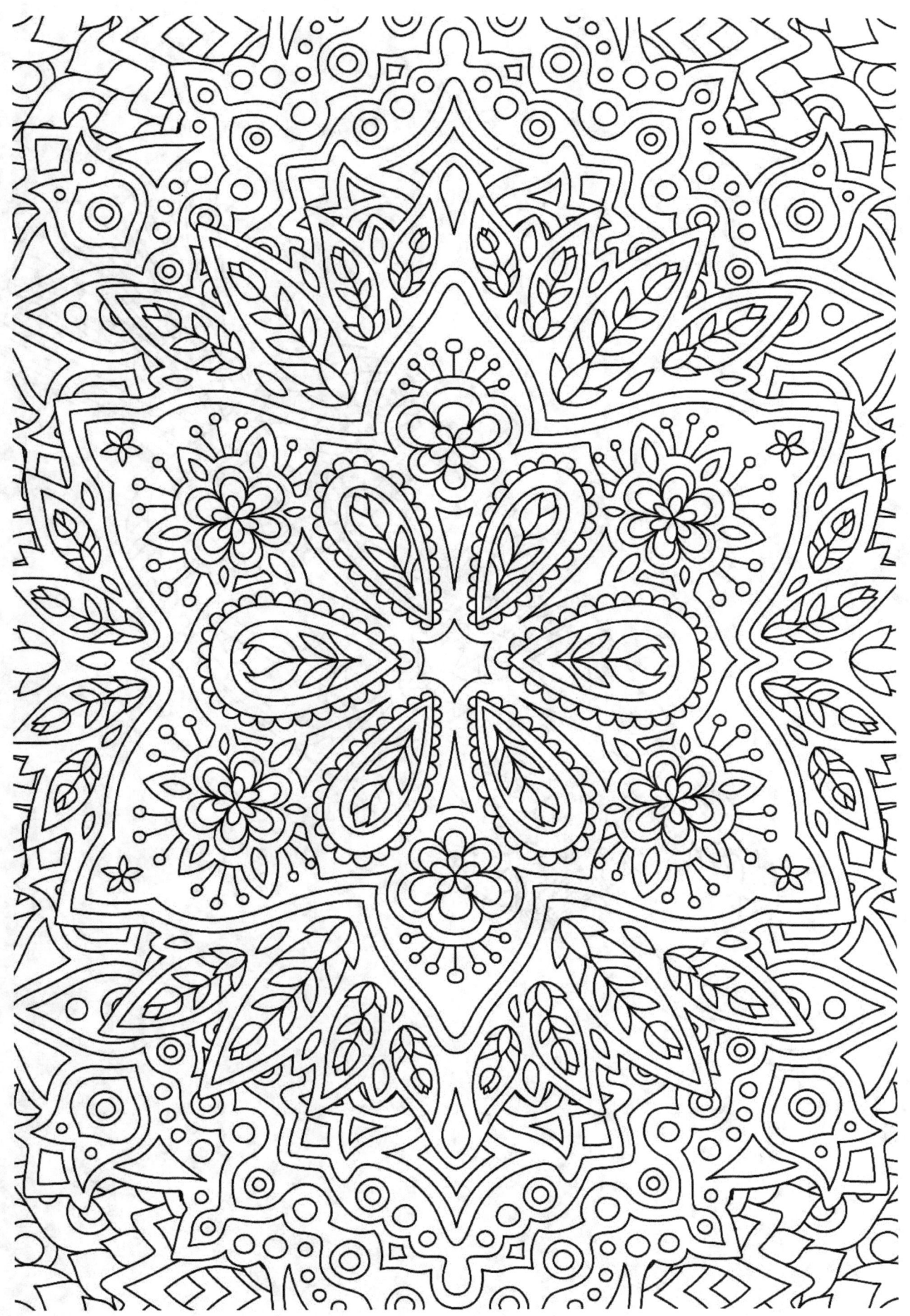

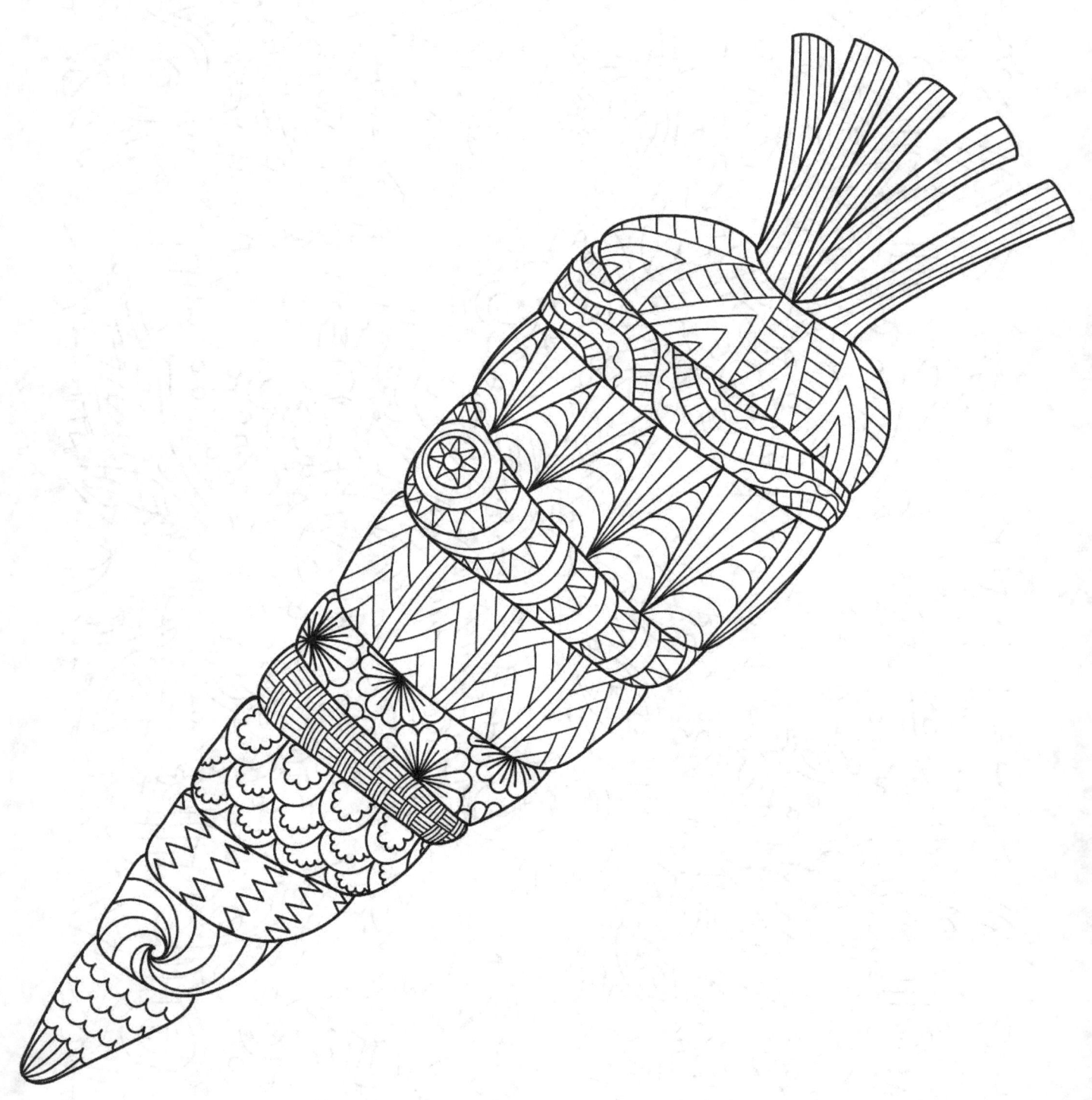

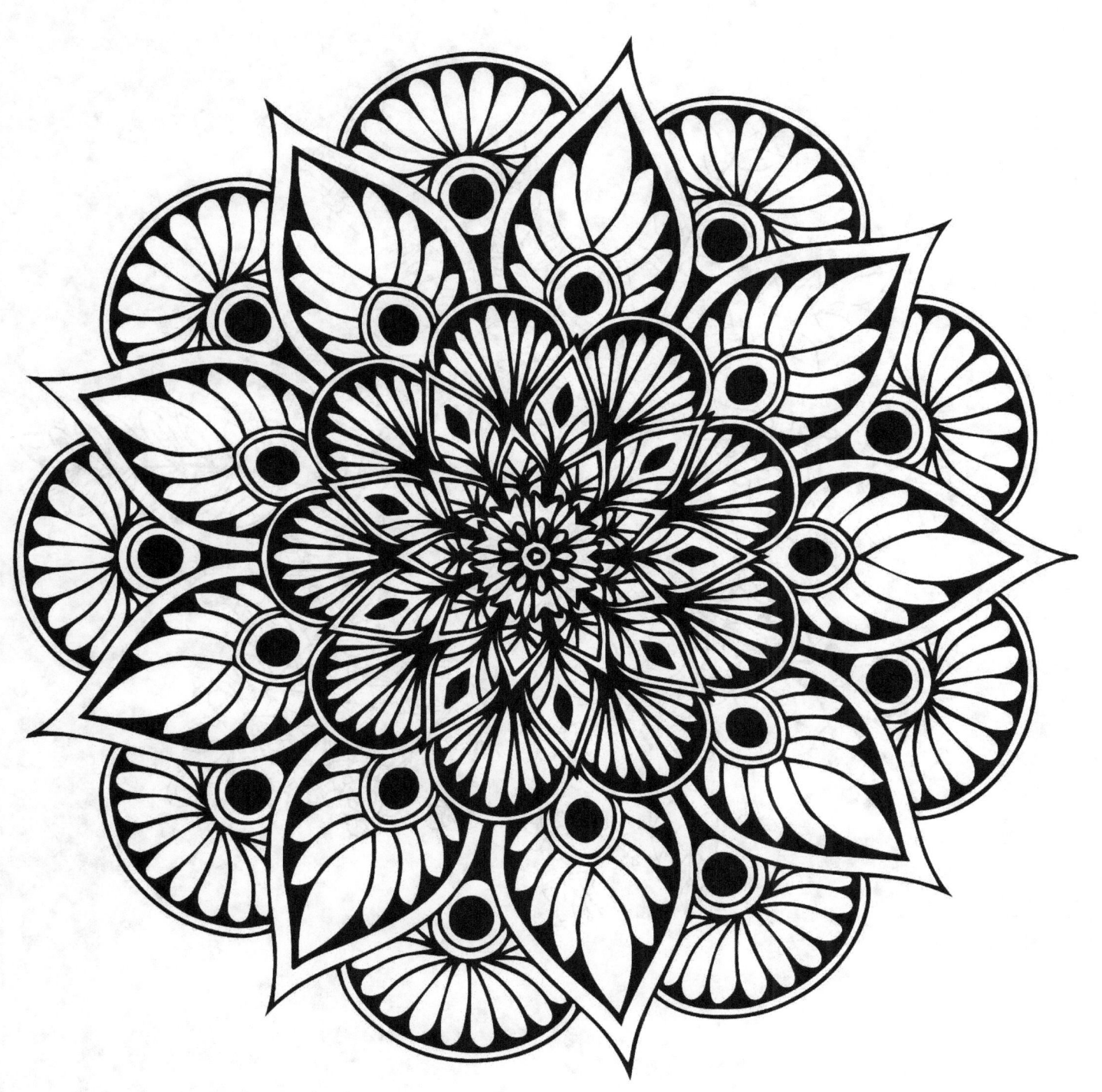

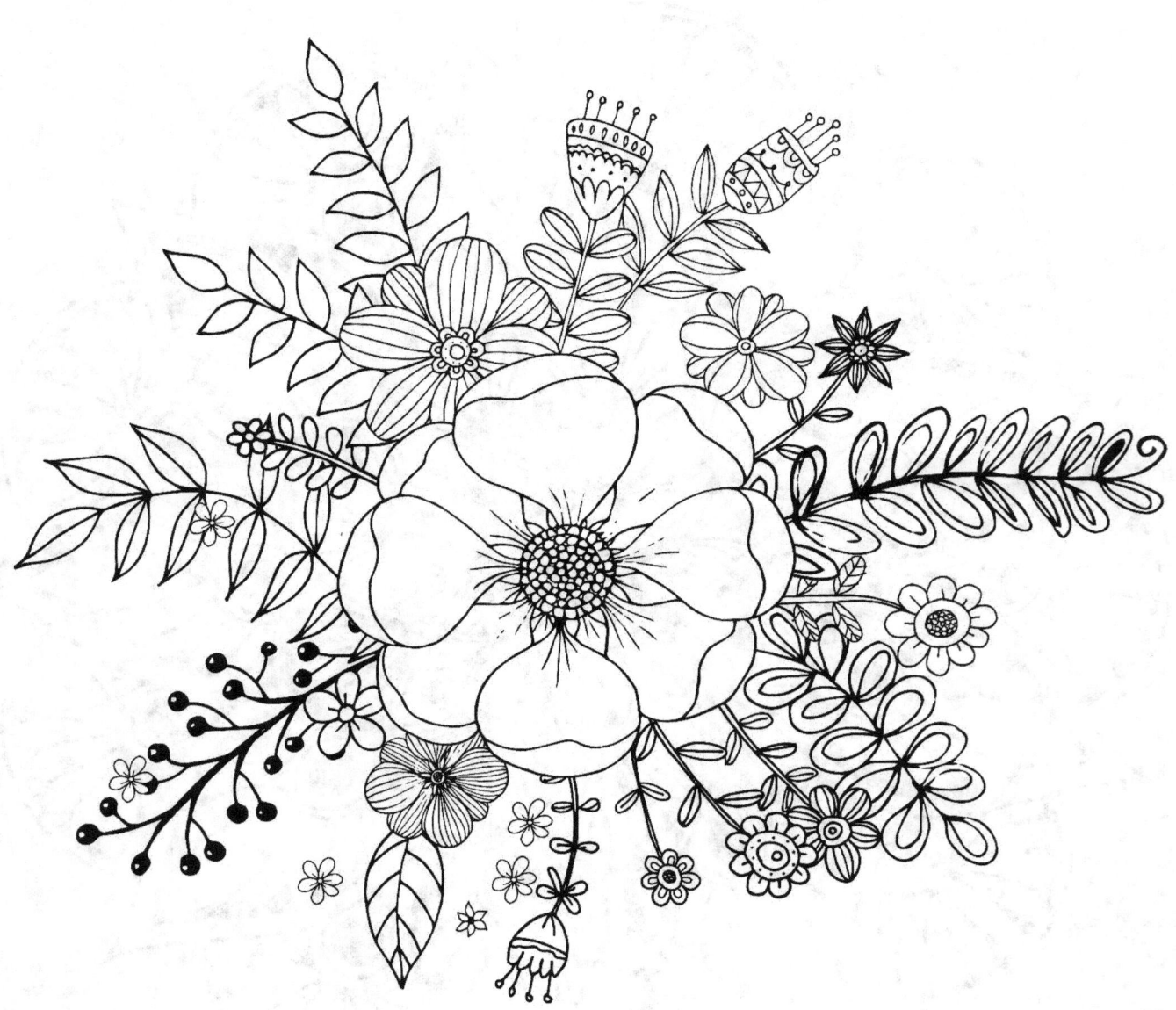

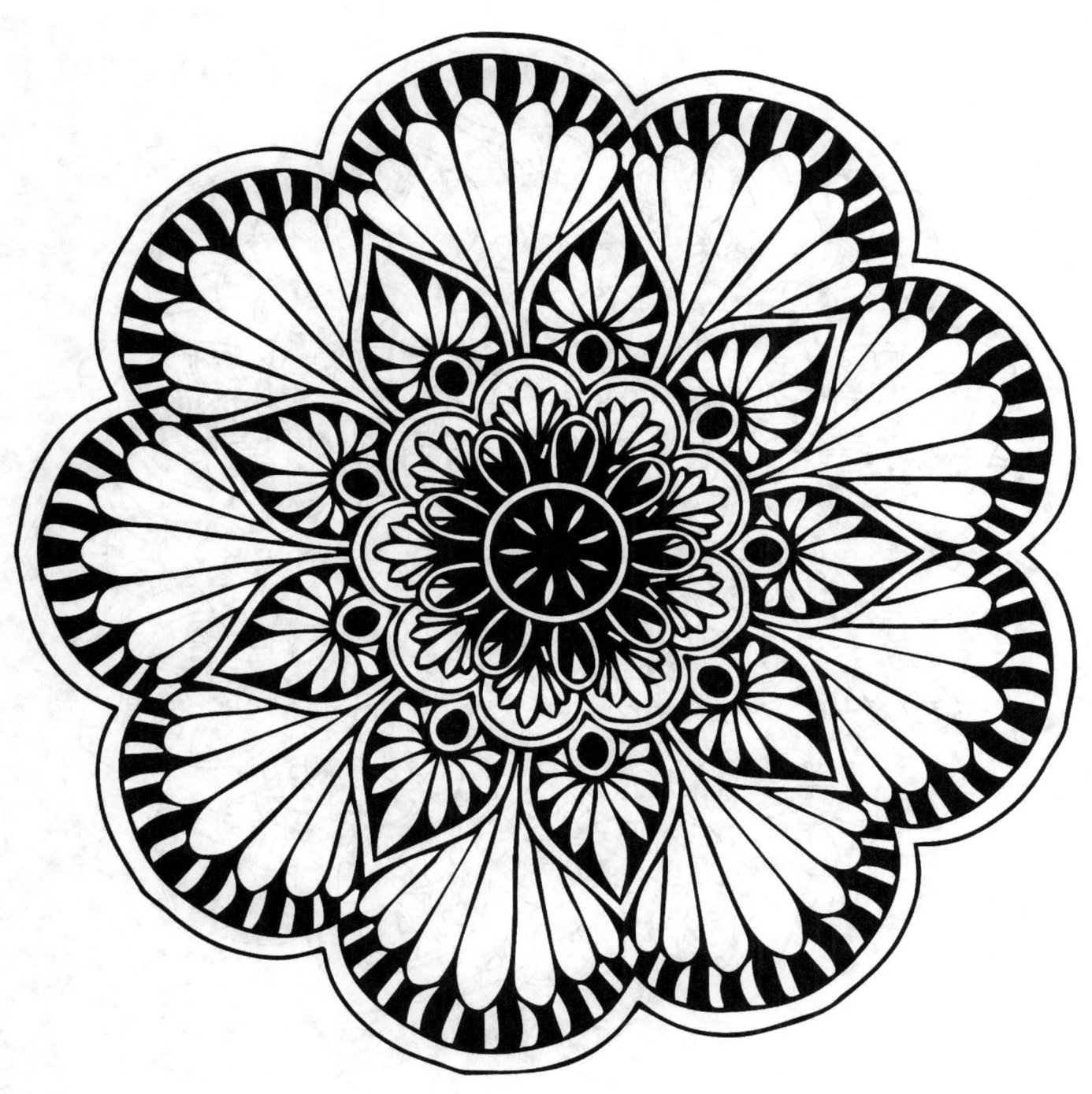

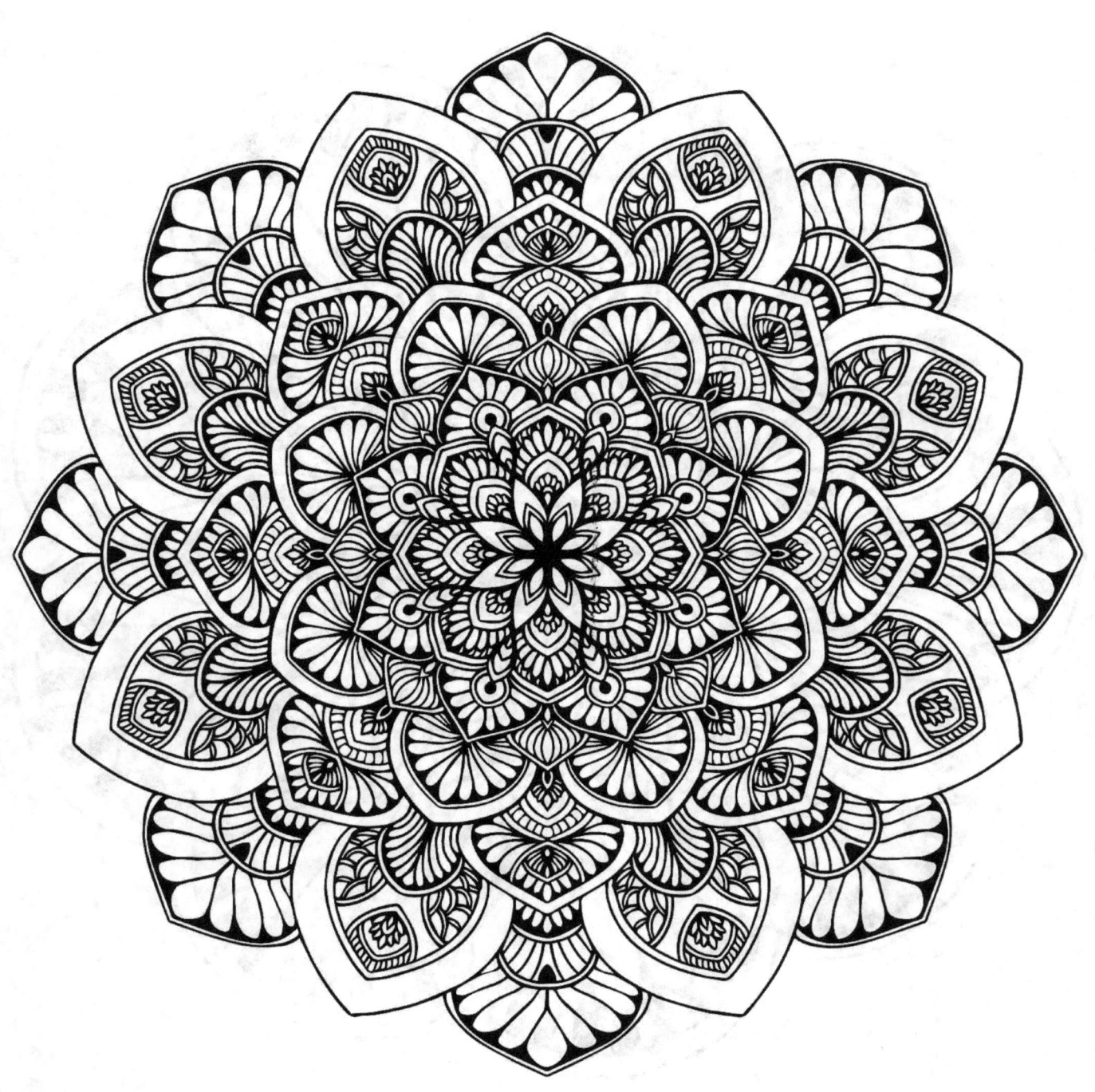

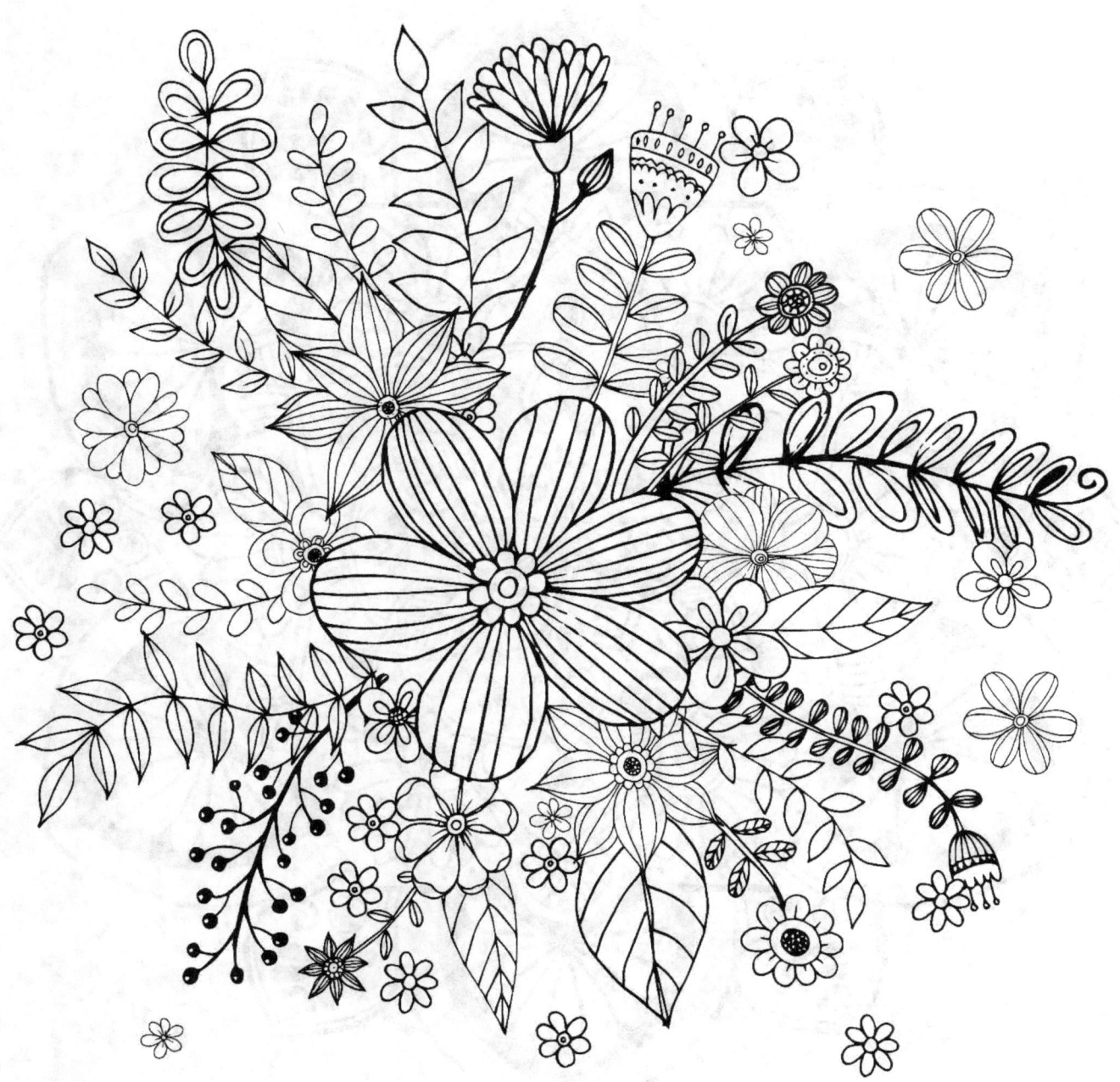

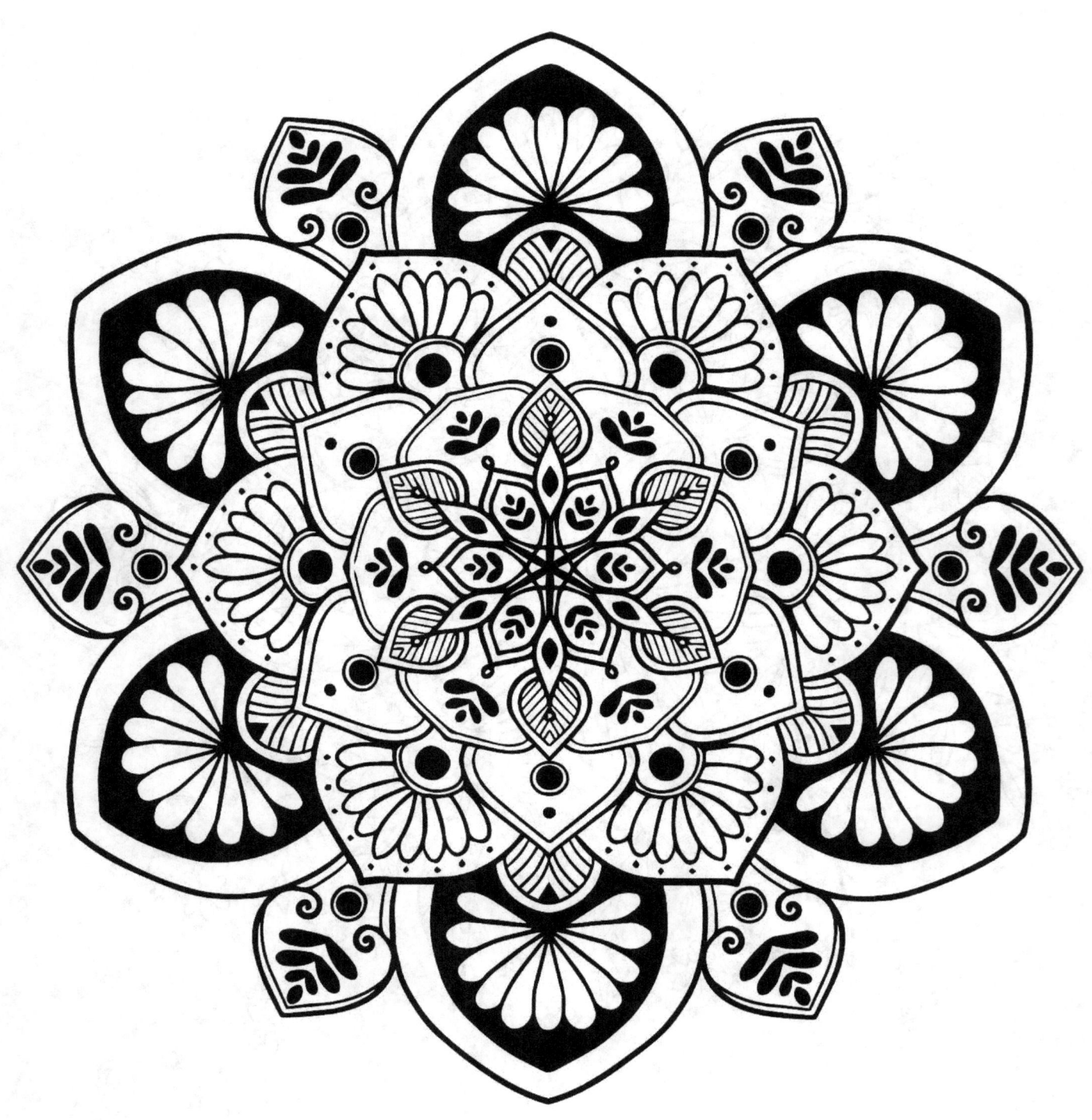

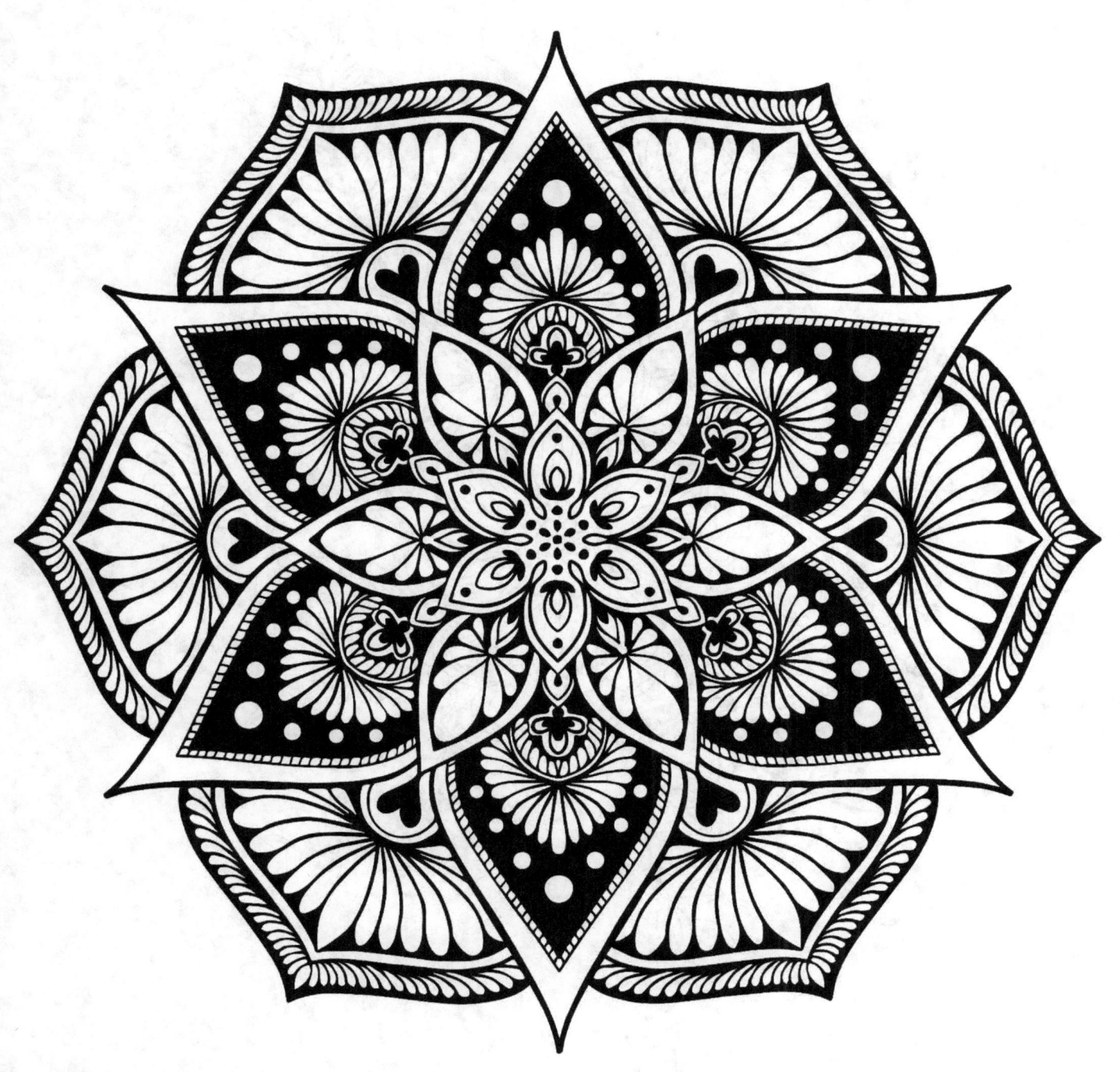

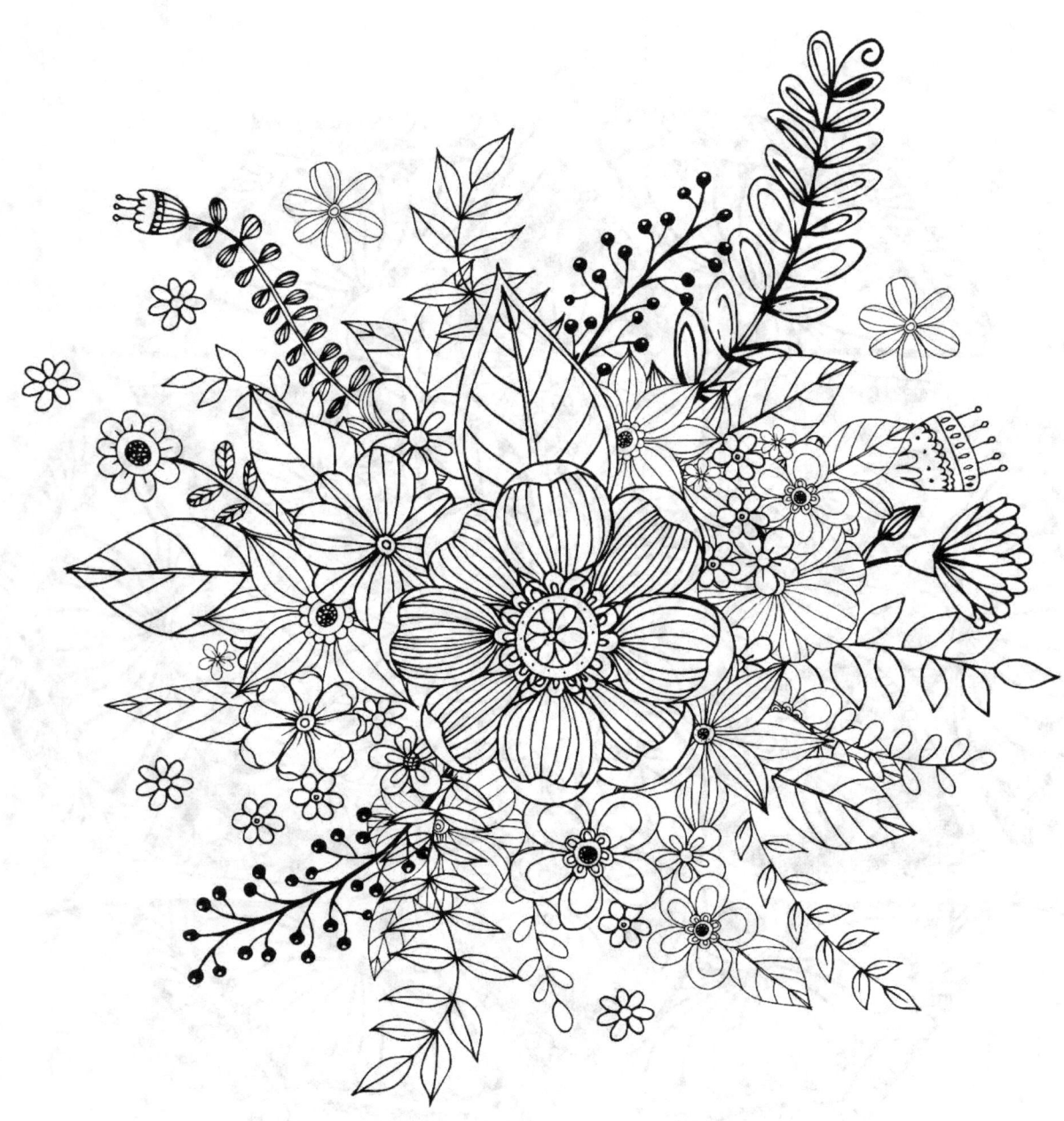

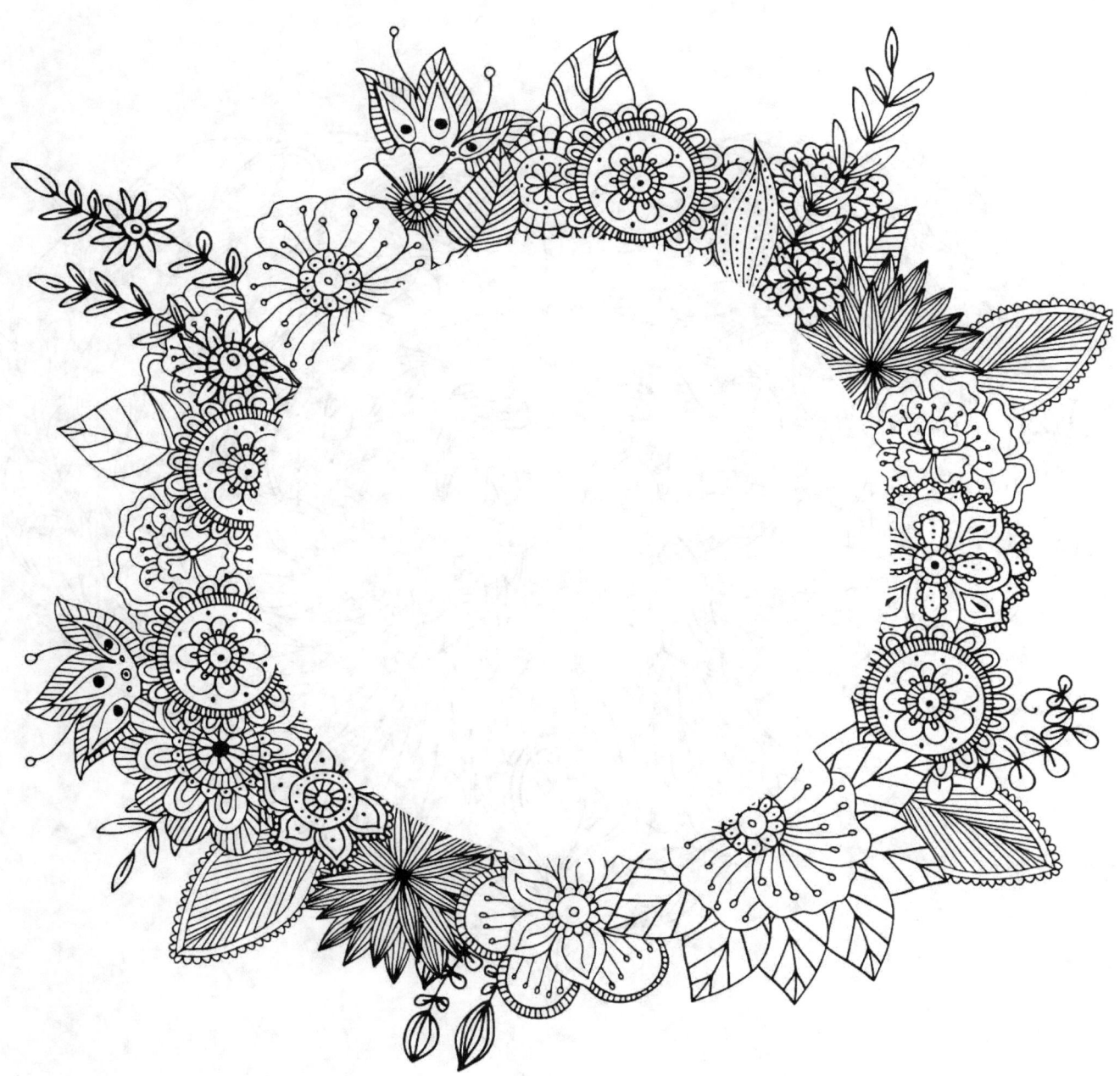

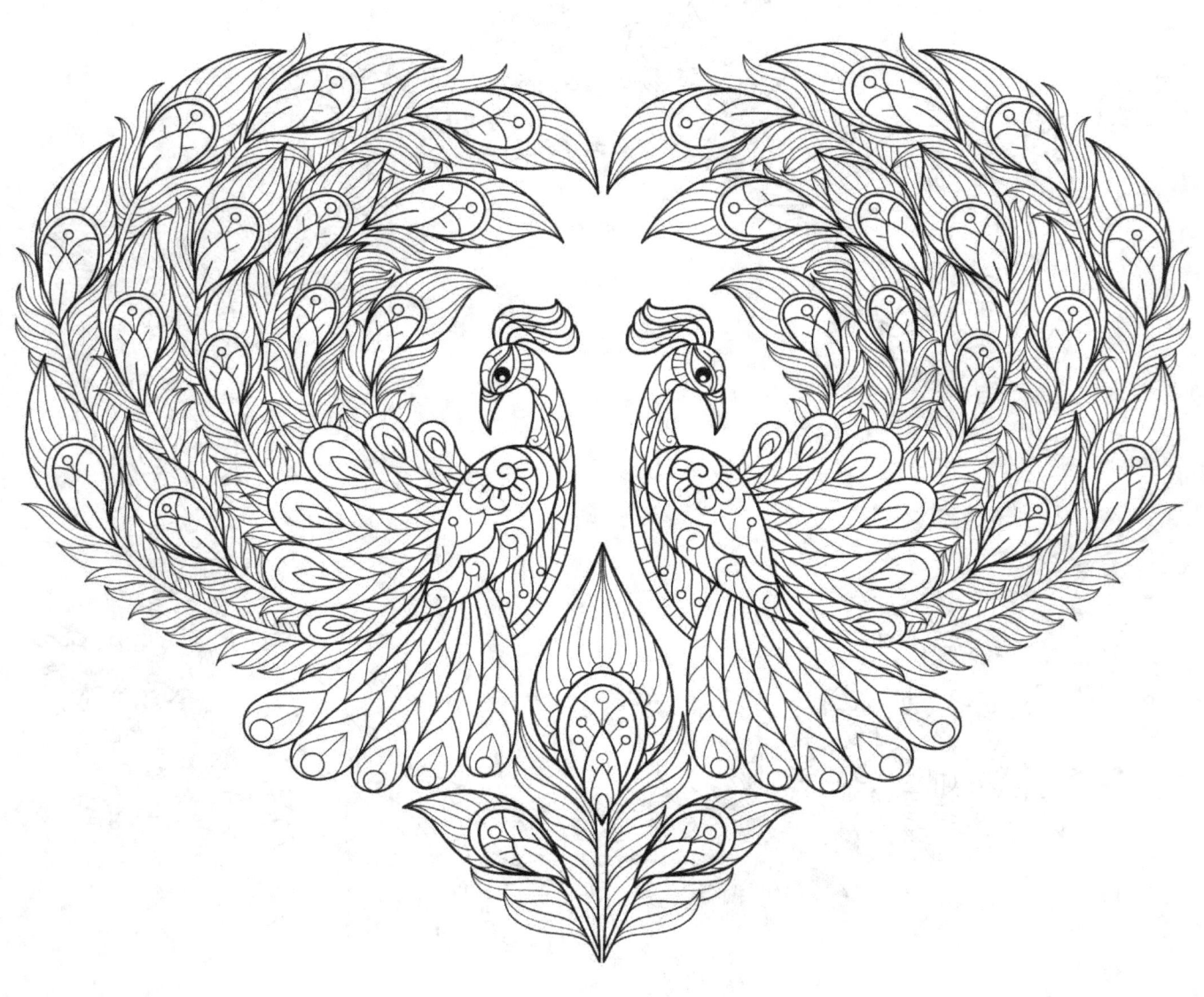

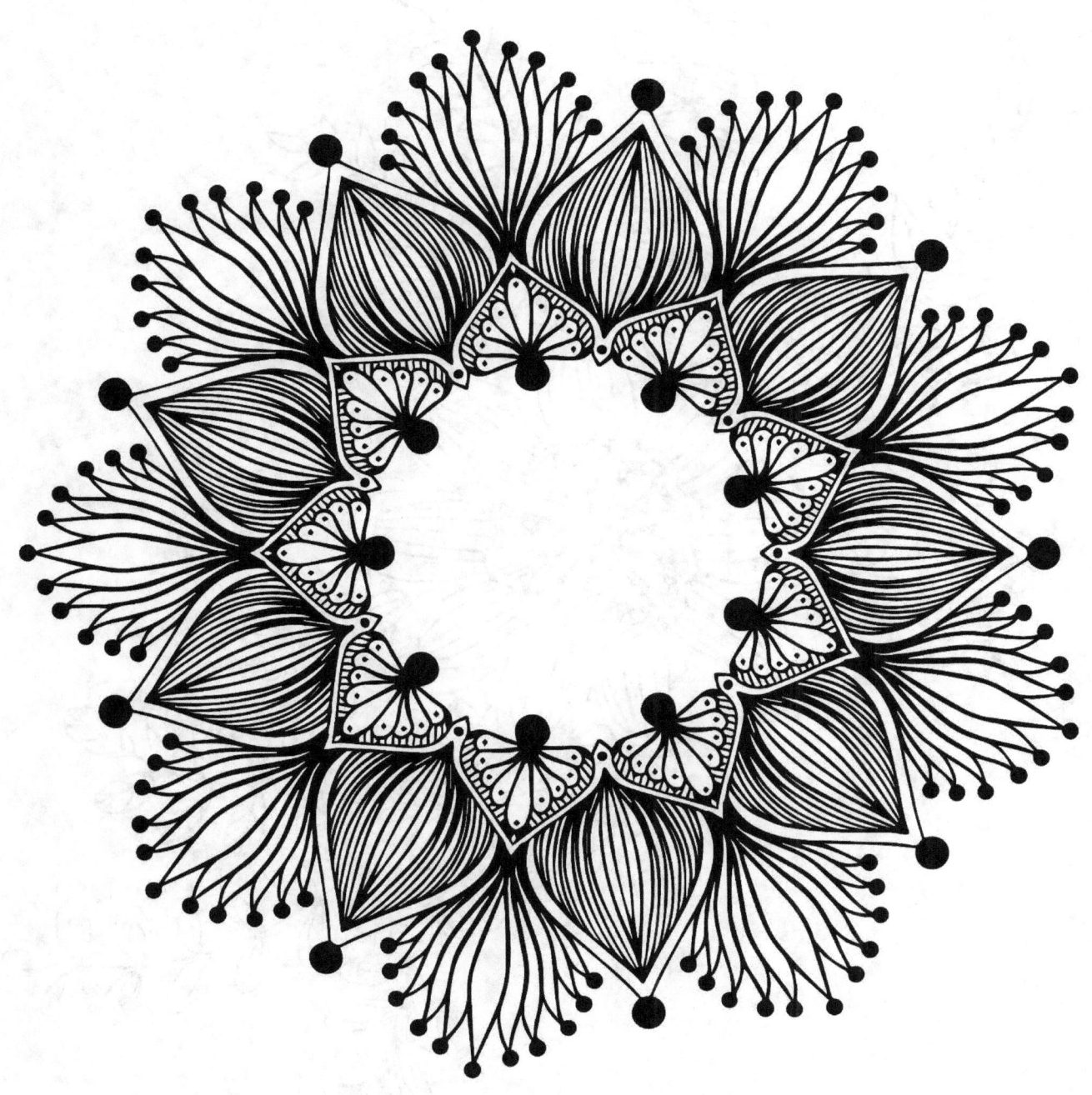

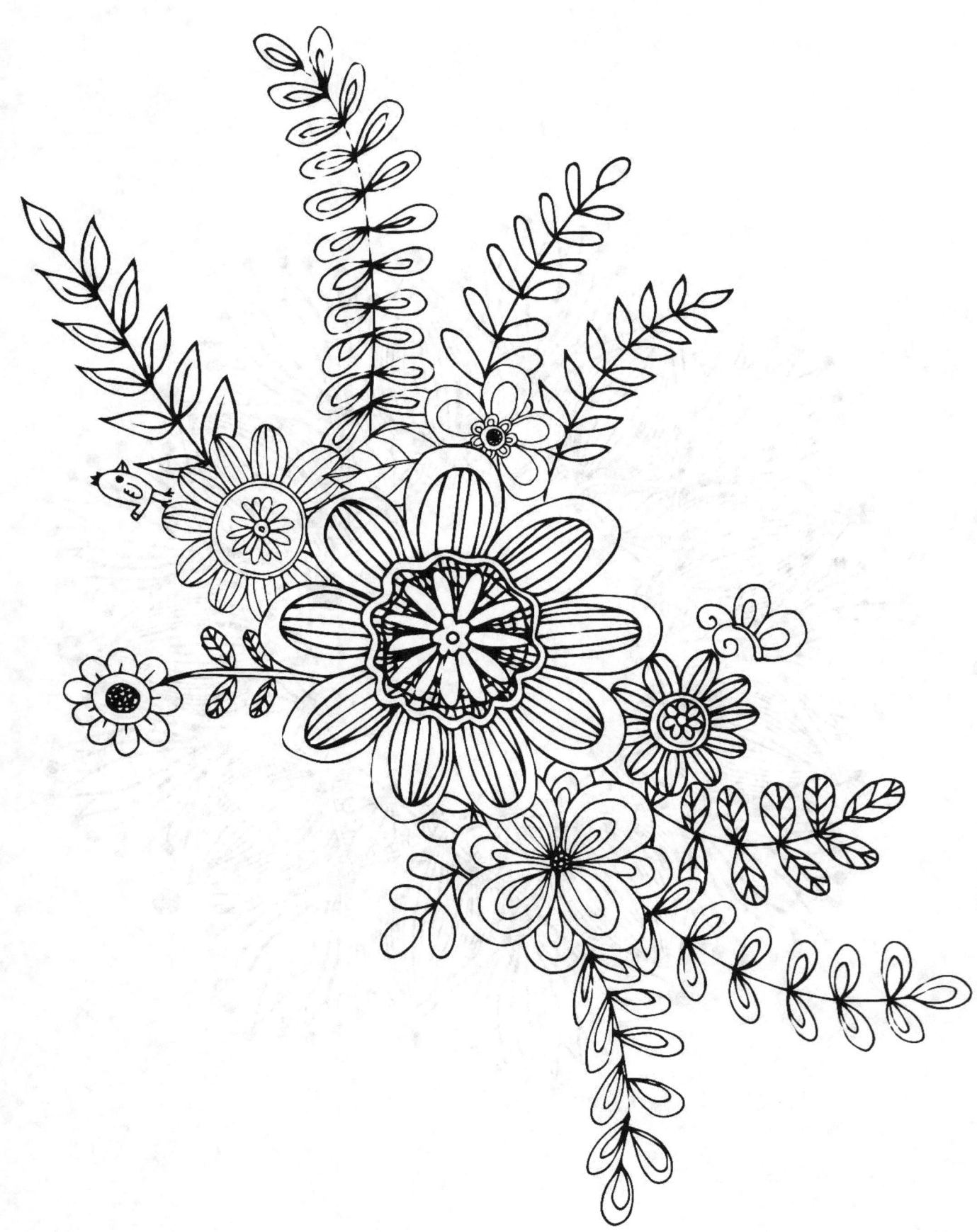

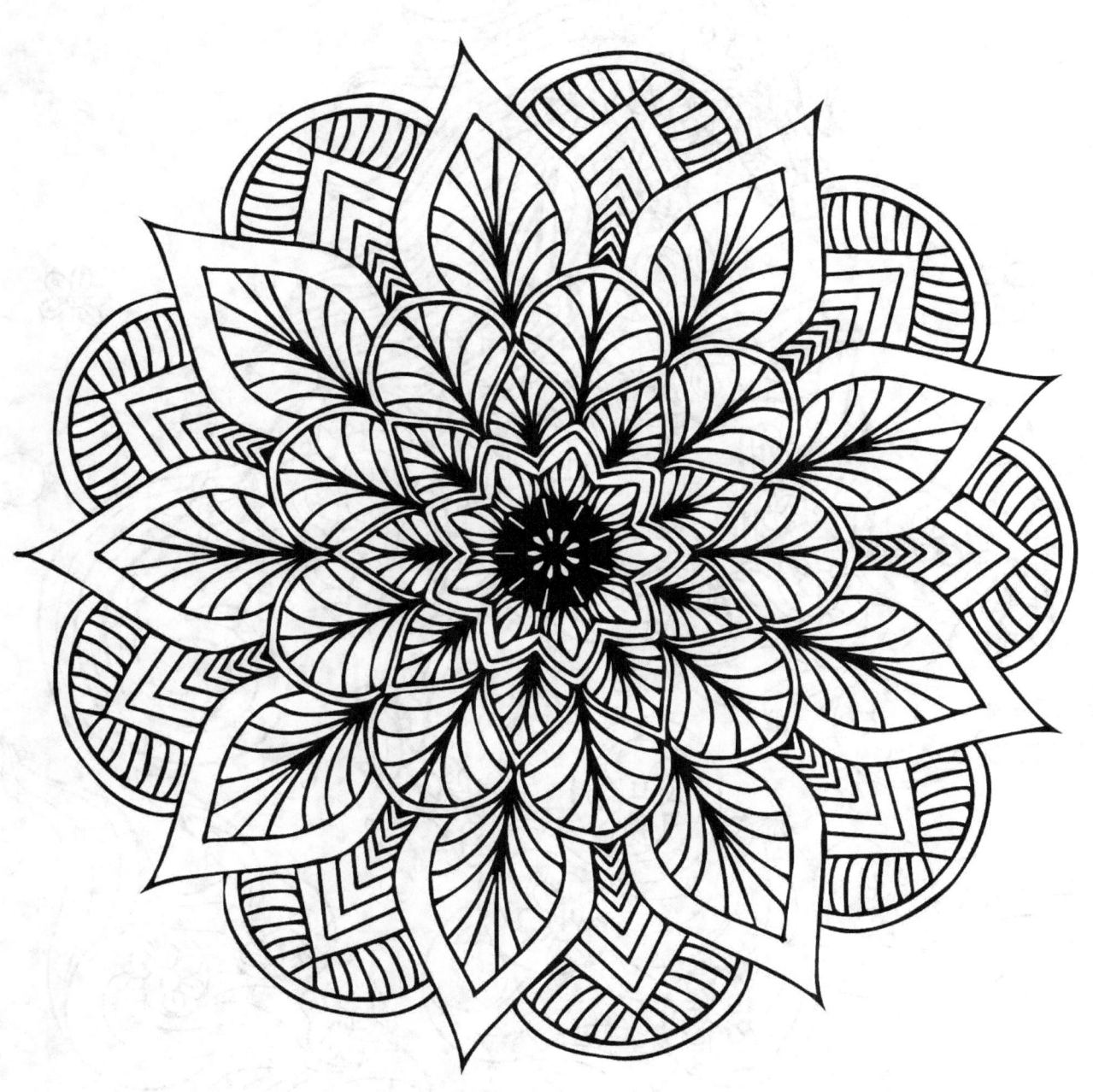

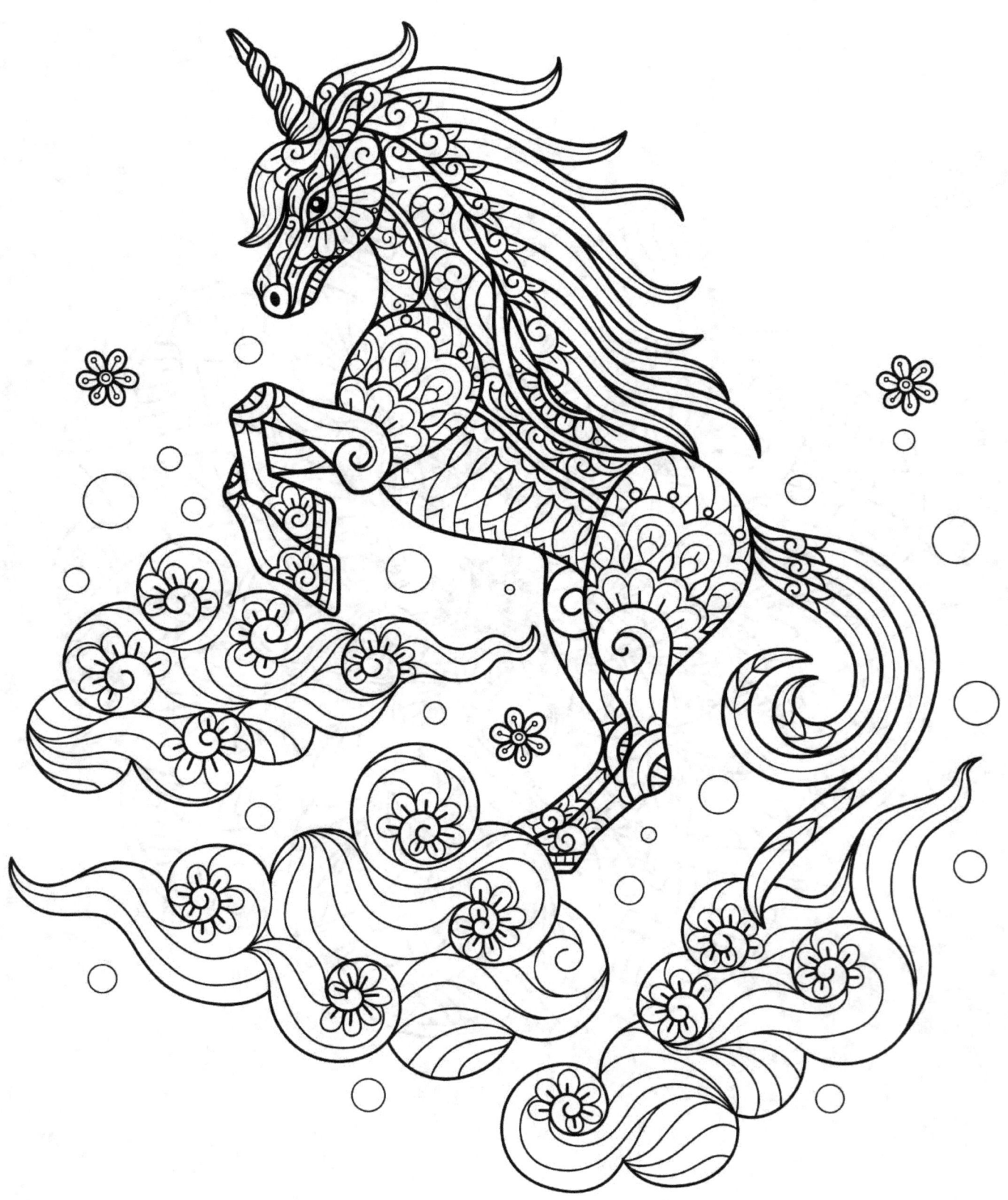

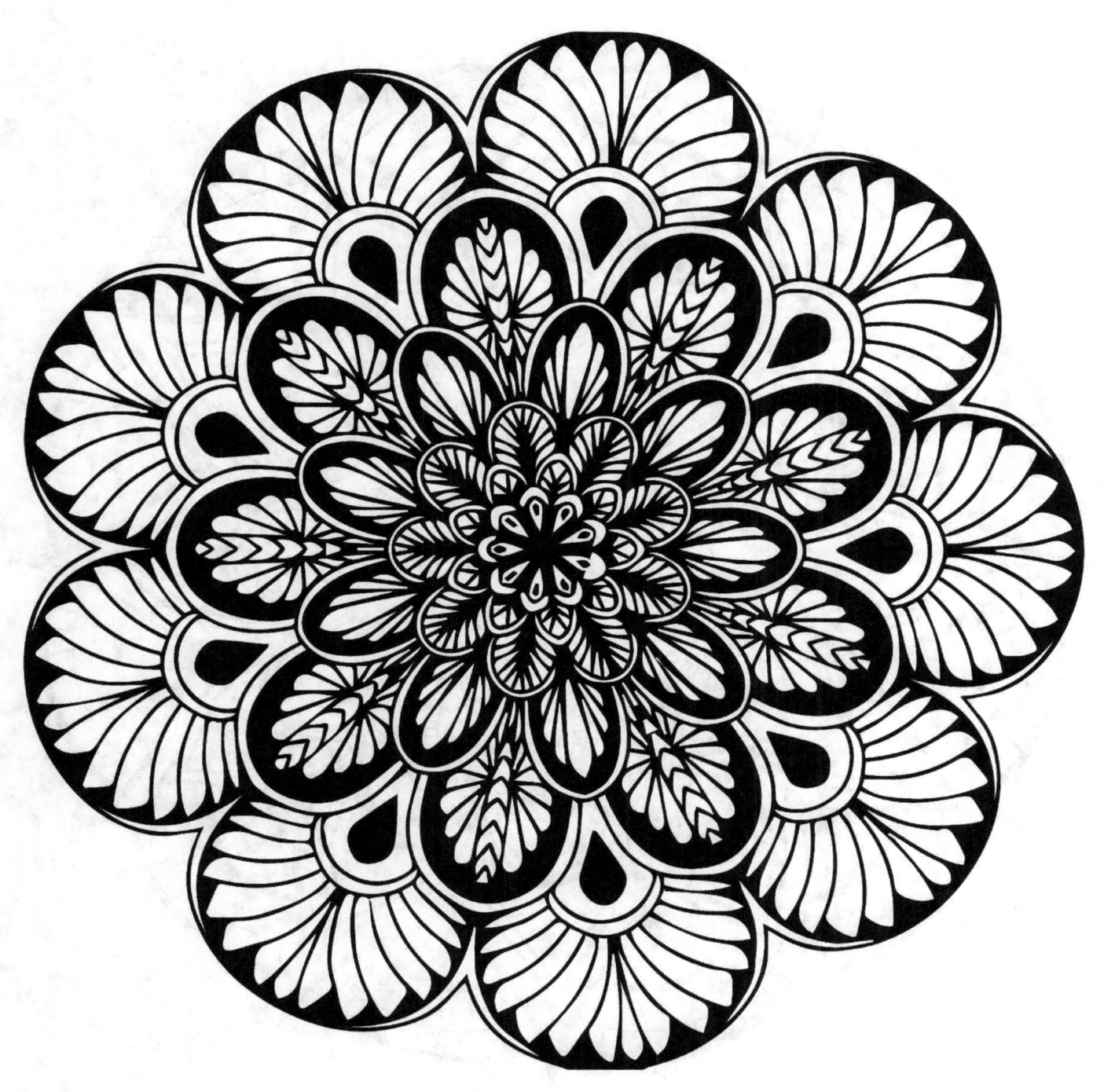

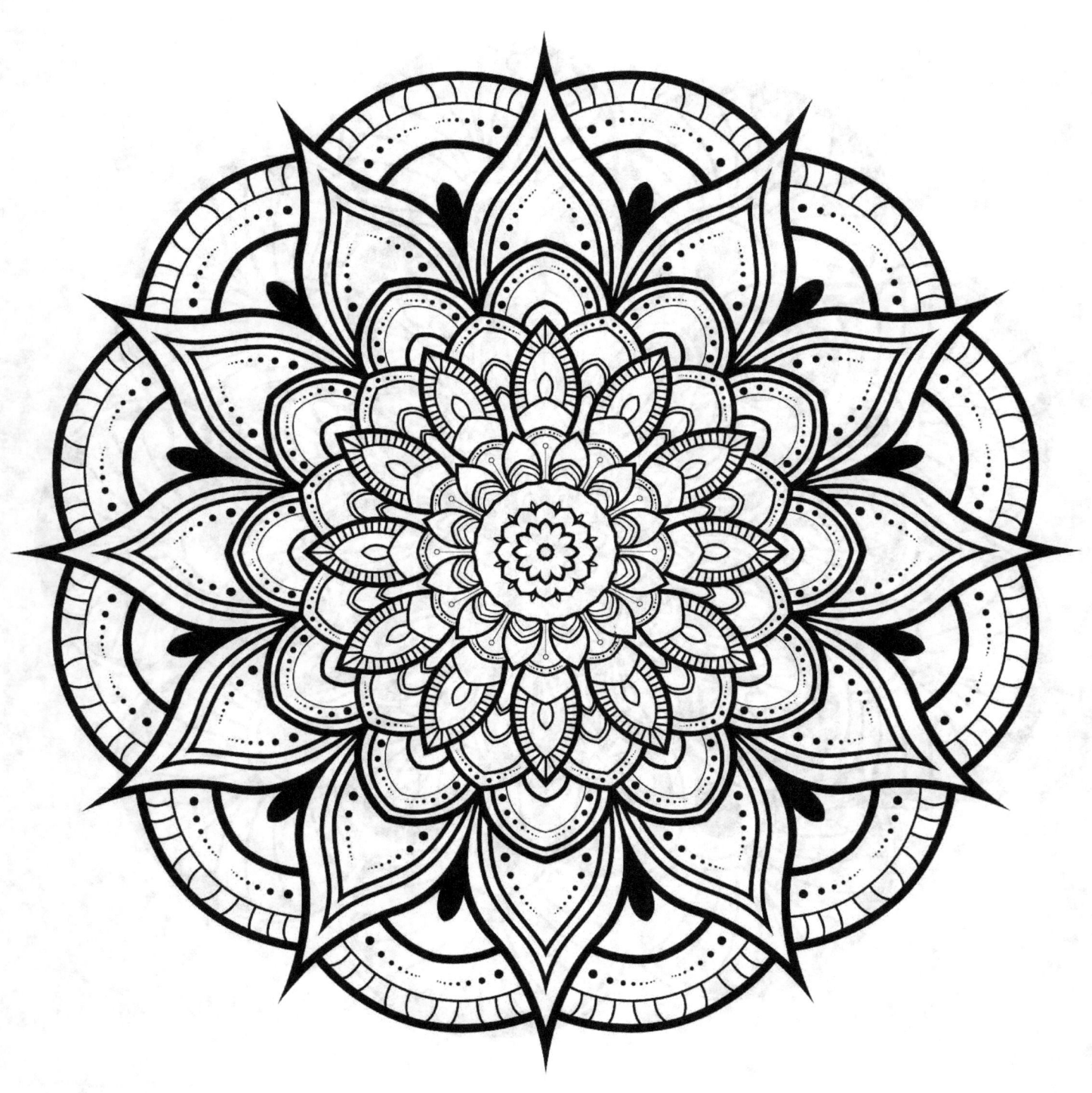

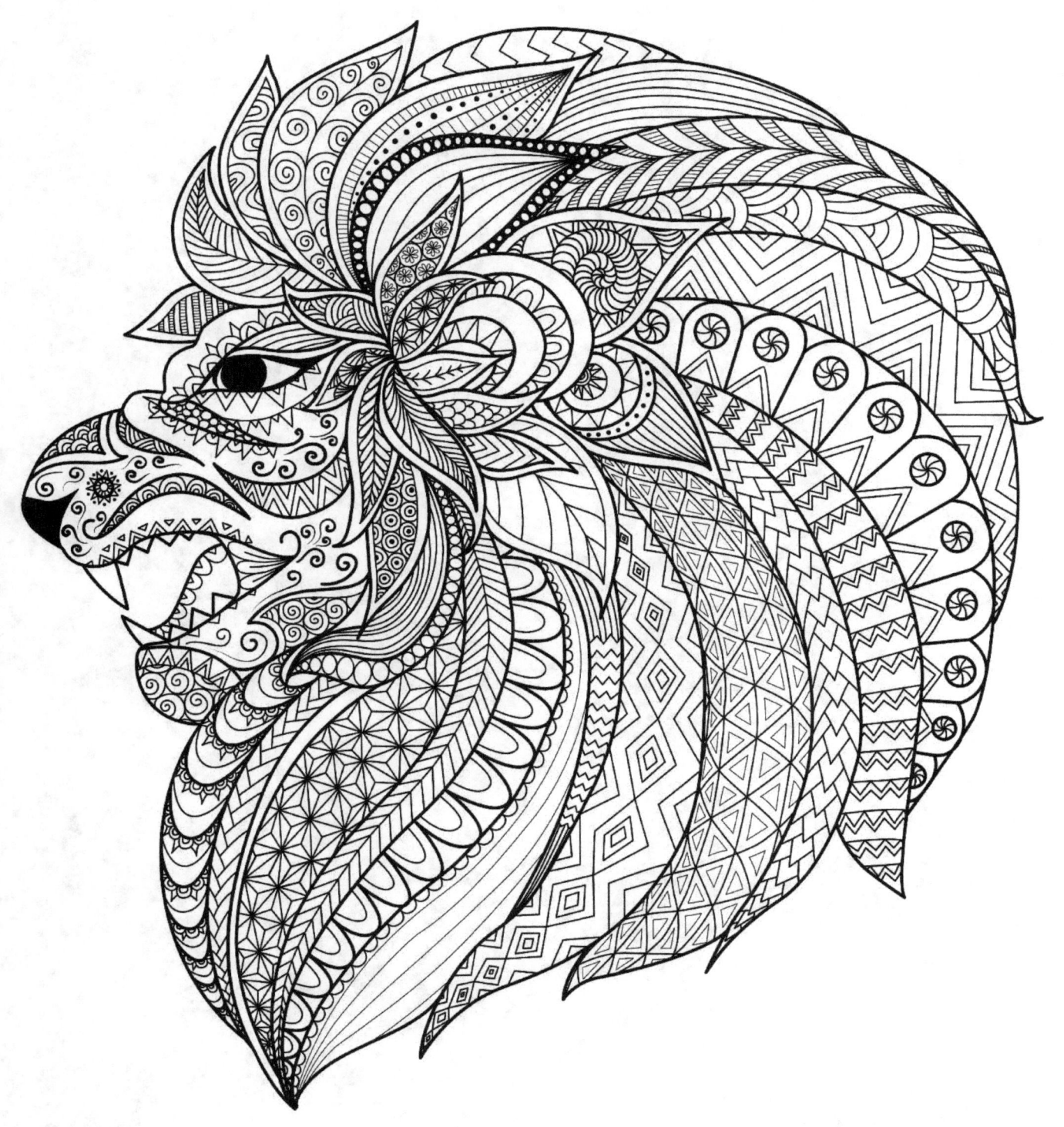

www.ingramcontent.com/pod-product-compliance
Lightning Source LLC
Chambersburg PA
CBHW060438220526

45465CB00008B/3186